DISCIPLE of C...
EDUCATION IN VIRTUE ™

LENTEN JOURNAL

By Sister John Dominic Rasmussen, O.P.

LUMEN ECCLESIAE
PRESS

Copyright © 2015 Education In Virtue. All rights reserved. No part of this publication may be reproduced or transmitted in any form or means, electronic or mechanical, including photocopy, recording, or information storage and retrieval system, without the permission in writing from the publisher.

Published by Lumen Ecclesiae Press
    4101 East Joy Road
    Ann Arbor, Michigan 48105

Catechism of the Catholic Church quotes are taken from the English translation of the *Catechism of the Catholic Church* for the United States of America copyright © 1994, United States Catholic Conference — Liberia Editrice Vaticana. English translation of the *Catechism of the Catholic Church*: Modification from the Edito Typica copyright © 1997, United States Catholic Conference, Inc. — Liberia Editrice Vaticana.

Scripture texts in this work are taken from the New American Bible, revised edition © 2010, 1991, 1986, 1970 Confraternity of Christian Doctrine, Washington, D.C. and are used by permission of the copyright owner. All Rights Reserved. No part of the New American Bible may be reproduced in any form without permission in writing from the copyright owner.

Cover Artwork: Illustration for *The Life of Christ*, Tissot, James Jacques Joseph / Brooklyn Museum of Art, New York, USA / Bridgeman Images

Back Cover Artwork: Illustration for *The Life of Christ*, Tissot, James Jacques Joseph / Brooklyn Museum of Art, New York, USA / Bridgeman Images

Inside Cover Artwork: Illustration for *The Life of Christ*, Tissot, James Jacques Joseph / Brooklyn Museum of Art, New York, USA / Bridgeman Images

Stations of the Cross Artwork: Illustration for *The Life of Christ*, Tissot, James Jacques Joseph / Brooklyn Museum of Art, New York, USA / Bridgeman Images

Book Design Layout: Linda Kelly
Cover Design: Amy Beers
Copy editor: Claudia Volkman
Copyrights and Permissions: Kristina Smith and Sally Wagner

Requests for permission to make copies of any part of the work should be directed to: info@educationinvirtue.com.

ISBN 978-0-9899921-4-5

First Printing
Printed in the United States of America

TABLE OF CONTENTS

Letter from Amy Grant..7

Letter from Matt Maher...8

Letter from Ike Ndolo..9

Introduction...11

Preparation for Lent..12

Plan for Lent..19

Disciple of Christ Virtue Chart...22

Lectio Divina: Living Lent with the Word..24

Gratitude Log..25

Letter from Audrey Assad...50

Letter from Matt Hammitt..61

Letter from Jon Guerra...82

Stations of the Cross...95

How to Use This Journal

The season of Lent begins on Ash Wednesday, February 18, 2015 and it is a time of embracing penance to draw near to Christ. The various parts of this journal are intended to help you love Jesus more and to live as a disciple of Christ.

 Preparation for Lent: The preparation for Lent section is intended to help you prepare for a fruitful Lent. Spend time reading the section and decide upon a Plan for Lent for yourself. Pray to the Holy Spirit to assist you in your personal reparation. (A teacher may wish to guide the students through the preparation.)

 Lectio Divina: Read the Gospel passage for each day of Lent. The questions are written to guide your prayerful reading of the Scripture.

 Gratitude Log: The gratitude log is included with each daily Scripture passage.

 Religious Artwork: The paintings have been selected to assist you in your meditations. Spend time prayerfully studying the images. You may wish to research the artist and the time period of the painting.

 Christian Witness Letters: Christian music artists have contributed letters to encourage you to live as disciple of Christ.

 Visual Journey of Christ's Passion: On Good Friday, a visual journey of Christ's passion has been included. This is an expansion of the Stations of the Cross. Let the beauty of these paintings enrich your meditation on the Passion.

A letter from Amy...

Lent 2015

Dear Disciple of Christ,

When I was in fifth grade, I began reading the Bible for myself because I was curious about Jesus. My mom had given me a modern translation of the Bible called Good News for Modern Man. It was a paraphrased version and written in a story form. My reading of the Good News was not a homework assignment, but the beginning of my journey of faith. As I read and re-read the Gospels, the eyes of my heart were opened, and I started to see the person of Jesus Christ. I treasured the quiet moments spent reading about His life and all He taught by word and example. This is how my relationship with Him began and has continued throughout my life.

As you spend the next forty days reading various Gospel passages, let this encounter be for yourself as you meet Jesus in the Word. Get to know the person of Jesus through the Gospels, and remember, this is not a homework assignment or something to "get done." It's about establishing a relationship with Jesus, who loves you immensely. Let His name—Jesus—be ever present in your mind and heart. When you can't think of anything else to say, speak His name, for He is the One who sustains us.

Amy Grant

UNITE. PRAISE. GIVE BACK.
AMY WILL BE PERFORMING ON 4.19.15 AT
THE UNITE - DISCIPLES OF CHRIST CONCERT.
UNITECONCERT.COM | AMYGRANT.COM

A letter from Matt...

Lent 2015

My Dear Young Disciples,

In 2002 St. John Paul II asked the young people at World Youth Day in Toronto, "Why have you come together from all parts of the world?" I ask you a similar question now: Why have so many of you, from all parts of the world, come to read these pages about being His disciple? St. John Paul II answered for the youth: "To say in your hearts: 'Lord, to whom shall we go?... You have the words of eternal life' (John 6:68). Jesus — the intimate friend of every young person — has the words of life."

As you read and reflect on the pages of this journal, know that thousands of other youth do the same. You are not alone. Jesus is right there with you, and He is your intimate friend. You are never alone. Perhaps His grace is so powerful and His presence so real that even through these pages His words of life can unite us: "Wherever two or more are gathered in my name, there am I in your midst" (Matthew 18:20).

Gather with me now, young disciples of Christ — let's pray through these pages together and unite our prayers, lifting our hearts and minds to God. Though physical proximity might seem to distance us, we can still come together from all parts of the world in prayer and praise and proclaim together, "Lord, to whom shall we go?" and "You have the words of eternal life." Then, in our own cities and in our own schools, we can be disciples of Christ, following our intimate Friend and bringing others to Him. Even so, if someday by His providence your discipleship path crosses that of another reading these pages, you will recognize each other by the walk walked and the talk talked...but most of all by the light in your eyes — His light.

Matt Maher

[signature]

UNITE. PRAISE. GIVE BACK.
MATT WILL BE PERFORMING ON 4.19.15 AT THE
UNITE - DISCIPLES OF CHRIST CONCERT.
UNITECONCERT.COM | MATTMAHERMUSIC.COM

A letter from Ike...

Lent 2015

Dear Disciple of Christ,

A little over a year ago, at the end of 2013, I lost my father to cancer. No one is fully prepared for the loss of someone so close. I was not prepared. My world as I knew it ceased to be and I was forced to live a new reality, to live in this new world. I struggled in my grief, I felt lost, abandoned, even betrayed by God. My friends and those close to me offered their kind words and condolences but they got to move on in a way that I could not. It was like losing a limb and figuring out how to function without it.

Lent of 2014 was one of the hardest times of my life. I walked into those forty days a broken man, hurting from the loss of my dad. But as I struggled, I carried a thought that brought me hope, death is not the end.

Lent is a journey that asks us to join in Christ's hardest moments here on earth. To enter that desert of sacrifice and suffering and walk with Him to the garden, and to the scourging pillar and ultimately to the Cross. Jesus, the Son of God, shares our humanity and everything that comes with it. He felt loneliness, and betrayal, he felt grief and sorrow. So we draw near to Him in our own times of trial and darkness and know He draws near to us. Do not let the forty days of lent pass you by, journey with purpose, share in Christ's passion. Stay with Him in the garden, stand with Him at the scourging pillar and do not leave Him at the Cross. Remember, death is not the end. By sharing in His suffering, we get to share in His glory. To become "Easter People" to rise with Christ on Sunday morning, we must first die with him on that Good Friday. Death is not the end

UNITE. PRAISE. GIVE BACK.
IKE WILL BE PERFORMING ON 4.19.15 AT THE
UNITE - DISCIPLES OF CHRIST CONCERT.
UNITECONCERT.COM | CURRENTMM.COM

Ike Ndolo

INTRODUCTION

"Whoever wishes to come after me must deny himself, take up his cross, and follow me. For whoever wishes to save his life will lose it, but whoever loses his life for my sake will find it."
(Matthew 16:24–25)

It is the first day of a new sports season. Everyone is excited, and the coach thinks the team has the potential to win the championship. Both the players and the coach know, though, that it will be a long time before they are ready to compete. The initial weeks on the team are rigorous because the athletes must get in shape in order to sustain the intensity of a competition. There will be long weeks of conditioning. The players spend countless hours practicing, working out, and growing in self-discipline before the first game.

St. Paul drew upon this example when he stated, "Every athlete exercises discipline in every way. They do it to win a perishable crown, but we an imperishable one" (1 Corinthians 9:25). Jesus was the first to sacrifice for this crown. Jesus humbled Himself by becoming a little child. He was obedient to Mary and Joseph, and although He was God, He allowed two human beings to guide His life while spending thirty years living the ordinary life of an Israelite. As a carpenter, He knew the pain of getting splinters in His hand and the backache after a hard day of work. Eventually Jesus was obedient unto death (Philippians 2:8); He suffered, was crucified, and was buried so that all might rise to eternal life with Him.

Every baptized person has been immersed in the Paschal Mystery of Christ — His passion, death, and resurrection. Like Christ, the Christian learns to make sacrifices for a higher good. There are times of discipline and growth, times of conditioning in order to win the crown of friendship with God. Jesus tells us, "Unless a grain of wheat falls to the ground and dies, it remains just a grain of wheat; but if it dies, it produces much fruit. Whoever loves his life loses it, and whoever hates his life in this world will preserve it for eternal life" (John 12:24–25). By dying to himself the Christian hopes to become more loving, more joyful, more merciful…more like God. This pattern of dying and rising again as a "new creation" (2 Corinthians 5:17) in Christ marks the journey of a disciple — one who is willing to "take up his cross daily and follow me" (Luke 9:23).

INTRODUCTION

The Beatitude, "Blessed are the pure of heart for they shall see God," enables us to focus on the purpose of Lent as a time set aside for all Christians to embrace conversion and actively strive to purify one's heart. The heart, in the biblical sense, means the center of one's being where the passions, intellect, and will converge. Therefore, in order for one to "see God," one's heart needs to be cleansed of sin and weakness. The conditioning of the heart for Christians results in interior penance [cf. *CCC* 1430–1433].

With this in mind, let us prepare a "fitness plan" for the heart in order to draw closer to our loving God. Remember this truth: He loves you not because you are good but because He is good. The purpose of Lent is not to please God or to get a reward, but rather to obtain interior freedom, peace, joy, and happiness — so you may "see God."

The next few pages are intended to be a guideline for you to assist you in carefully examining yourself and your lifestyle. Pray for the gift of self-knowledge in order to recognize an area of your heart which needs "conditioning."

Courtesy of Debbie Herbeck

PREPARATION FOR LENT

THREE FORMS OF PENANCE

Fasting	Refraining from food and drink as an expression of interior penance, in imitation of how Jesus fasted for forty days in the desert. Fasting is an ascetical practice recommended in Scripture and the writings of the Church Fathers; it is sometimes prescribed by a precept of the Church, especially during the liturgical season of Lent (see *CCC*, 538, 1434, 2043).
Prayer	The elevation of the mind and heart to God in praise of his glory; a petition made to God for some desired good, or in thanksgiving for a good received, or in intercession for others before God. Through prayer the Christian experiences a communion with God through Christ in the Church (see *CCC*, 2559–2565).
Almsgiving	Money or goods given to the poor as an act of penance or fraternal charity. Almsgiving, together with prayer and fasting, are traditionally recommended to foster the state of interior penance (see *CCC*, 1434; cf. 1969, 2447).

Fasting

While fasting has traditionally been associated with refraining from food and drink, it is not limited to it. It can also include refraining from any activity you indulge in or derive pleasure from. Therefore, it is a means to strike an interior balance and master the desires of the world, pleasures of the flesh, and temptations of the devil.

Seeking to live virtuously assists the formation of good habits; that is, dispositions which enable you to properly order and harmonize your life in Christ. To determine how you can embrace fasting, quietly pause and reflect upon your daily life and patterns of behavior. The charts on the following pages are intended to be general and to serve as a starting point. The questions are designed to help you reflect on where you need to limit the excess in your life in order to be freed from a sinful habit (vice).

PREPARATION FOR LENT

Questions for self-reflection	Virtue to be cultivated	Ways to cultivate	Opposing trait
What activities consume a great deal of your time? How long do you spend on each? Are you able to say "no" when people pressure you to do something? Is there anything you cannot do without? Do you eat/drink more than you should?	**TEMPERANCE (SELF-CONTROL)**	Give up: - an activity which consumes your time - buying songs for your playlist or other media - a drink/food you regularly consume - snacking between meals	**Intemperance, over-indulging in a good thing**
How many hours do you sleep? Bedtime _____ Time you rise _____ Do you eat three healthy meals a day? Is your room/closet/dresser in order? Do you make your bed every morning?	**ORDERLINESS**	Go to bed at a reasonable time. Eat three healthy meals a day. Make your bed each day. Clean your room/car regularly.	**Disordered lifestyle** **Unhealthy eating habits** **Lack of proper sleep**
Do you waste time doing things you shouldn't be doing? Do you delay or "put off" doing chores or homework? Are you easily distracted when doing tasks? Do you deliberately distract others?	**INDUSTRIOUSNESS**	Make a plan for the day/week. Place a holy card on your desk to remind you to be diligent and focused at your labors. Do your chores first each day.	**Lack of motivation, being lazy**
Do you gossip or speak negatively of others? Do you text negative messages about people? Do you spread rumors?	**JUSTICE**	Refrain from speaking ill of others. Ask yourself if what you are going to say is true, kind, and helpful.	**Failing to see what is owed to each by virtue of his or her dignity**

PREPARATION FOR LENT

Questions for self-reflection	Virtue to be cultivated	Ways to cultivate	Opposing trait

What sort of casual activity do you engage in on your electronic devices?
 	
How much time do you spending using:
  - social media (Facebook)
  - video games, texting
  - interactive games
  - computer programs
  - listening to music
  - watching TV/movies
 	
Do any of these images or sounds disturb or distract you?
 	
Do they interfere with your ability to be pure of heart and mind?
 	
Does a song or image stay in your mind for a long time?
 	
How many songs do you have on your playlist?
 	
Is there a particular drink, food, or candy you enjoying having several times during the day?
 	
How much time do you spend working out (exercising)?
 	
How much of your day is given to socializing and hanging out with friends? Is it balanced?
	MODERATION	Refrain from listening to your favorite songs.
		
		Limit your posts or Internet time.
		
		Limit use of:
		- iPod
		- video games
		- consumption of energy drinks or beverages
		- movies, TV shows
			Giving in to being excessive in one or more areas of your life

PREPARATION FOR LENT

Questions for self-reflection	Virtue to be cultivated	Ways to cultivate	Opposing trait
Do you have to be the center of attention? Do you call out in class or interrupt others when they talk? Do you try to "one-up" others?	**HUMILITY**	Don't talk over others or interrupt them. Let others be recognized. Think before you speak. Ask yourself if it is: True, kind, and helpful. Allow others to tell the story first.	**Failing to recognize the gifts of others; being proud**
Do you view impure images on the Internet, TV, or in magazines? Do you read novels that have impure content? Do you dress in a way that reflects your dignity?	**MODESTY**	Guard your eyes; don't watch shows or read materials that you know are impure. Every time you use the computer, say a Hail Mary, Our Father, and Glory Be. Place holy cards around your computer (remember God is there). Say a Hail Mary every time you see something that is impure. Ask your parents or a trustworthy friend what they think if you are unsure if what you are wearing is modest.	**Choosing to dress or act in a way inconsistent with your dignity as a child of God**

PREPARATION FOR LENT

Prayer

Prayer is our means of communication with God. As disciples of Christ we are called to have a personal encounter with the person of Jesus Christ. The best comparison to developing a prayer life is a friendship. Our friends are people we can be completely honest with because we know that they are trustworthy. Friends have proven their love for us and will stand by us in good times and bad. They are the people we want to spend time with and with whom we can share whatever is in our heart. Prayer is the art of trusting God as we trust our closest friends. It is spending time with God, listening to Him speak to us and sharing with Him whatever is in our heart.

The Church says prayer is a form of penance. It is not always easy to trust God, as prayer always presupposes effort (see *CCC*, 2725–2758). We might fight against ourselves in prayer — against distractions, laziness, and temptations to stop trying. Unlike a merely human friendship, we don't always see the results of our prayers. For this reason it is tempting to give up. Pope Francis writes in his exhortation *Evangelii Gaudium* that it may be that God uses our sacrifices and prayers "to shower blessings in another part of the world which we will never visit. The Holy Spirit works as he wills, when he wills and where he wills; we entrust ourselves without pretending to see striking results. We know only that our commitment is necessary.... Let us keep marching forward; let us give him everything, allowing him to make our efforts bear fruit in his good time" (279).

Use the chart below to help you reflect on your life of prayer.

Questions for self-reflection	Virtue to be cultivated	Ways to cultivate	Opposing trait
Do you make your actions a prayer? Do you try to make your life a living prayer? Do you thank God for His blessings?	GRATITUDE	Look at the beauty of creation every day (one thing) and thank God for giving us this gift. Thank God daily for your life and its many blessings.	**Not expressing appreciation; taking other people and things for granted**
Do you pray during the time you have scheduled for prayer?	LOYALTY	Make a faithful commitment to daily prayer.	**Breaking bonds of trust with church, family, country, friends, and school**

-16-

PREPARATION FOR LENT

Questions for self-reflection	Virtue to be cultivated	Ways to cultivate	Opposing trait
Do you "offer up" annoyances or inconveniences? Do you pray for those who wrong you or annoy you? Do you pray with the Scriptures? Do you spend time in Eucharistic Adoration? Do you pray for others? Do you ask God to make you a better person?	**PRAYERFULNESS**	Look for places where you can be alone with God without distractions. Be still, offer up annoyances, pray for those who wrong you. Pray for others and for yourself.	**Entertaining distractions during prayers and Mass**
Do you schedule time for prayer every day?	**RESPONSIBILITY**	Responsibly schedule a time for prayer (right before you go to bed or in the morning).	**Failing to accept responsibility for your words and/or actions; being unreliable**
Do you speak with Jesus from your heart?	**HONESTY**	Share your heart with Jesus, recognizing that He "sees the heart."	**Being dishonest in words and actions; telling lies**
How do you spend Sundays? How do you spend Holy Days?	**JUSTICE**	Properly observe Sundays during Lent. Rest, do something you enjoy doing, and pray.	**Failing to see what is owed to each by virtue of his or her dignity**
Do you pray to "just get through" your prayer time? Do you ask God for the grace to be a better person?	**SINCERITY**	Be sincere in your prayer.	**Speaking or acting in a manner only to make yourself look good; being insincere**
Do you listen and wait for God's response? Do you seek immediate consolations in prayer? Do you give up when God doesn't answer as you want?	**PERSEVERANCE**	Be quiet in God's presence. Don't give up when prayer is hard...keep trying.	**Quickly giving up when a task is challenging**

PREPARATION FOR LENT

Almsgiving

" . . . man, who is the only creature on earth which God willed for itself, cannot fully find himself except through a sincere gift of himself." (GS, 24)

Almsgiving is often associated with donating money to worthy causes. This is one type of almsgiving, but the biblical understanding of almsgiving is much broader. Jesus says that when we "give for alms those things that are within," our hearts are purified (see Luke 11:41).

Prayerfully consider your daily life and patterns of behavior. Do you regularly give of your time and talents to others? Use the chart below to reflect on how you give alms.

Questions for self-reflection	Virtue to be cultivated	Ways to cultivate	Opposing trait
Do you look for opportunities to help others?	**MAGNIFICENCE**	Give generously of your time to others. Save some of the money you would have spent on songs, clothes, etc., and give it to the poor, your church, or a worthy organization.	Being wasteful; not responding to grace
Do you do your chores or clean up without being asked? Do you volunteer at your parish or school?	**MAGNANIMITY**	Do more than is expected of you. Surprise your siblings by doing their chores for them. Volunteer at your local parish.	Seeking to do great things for self-promotion — not seeking to do the good that is possible — pusillanimity (weak, spineless)
Do you seek out those who are being excluded and include them?	**GENEROSITY**	Seek out those who are being left out and invite them to hang out with you.	Giving without a spirit of cheer, with a begrudging manner
How much time do you spend with others? With your siblings? Do you intentionally exclude others?	**KINDNESS**	Be welcoming to others. Spend more time with your siblings. Spend the time you would have spent on the computer helping your parents.	Not regarding the well-being of others; being cruel in looks, words, and actions
Are you willing to help others? Do you complain when you have to do work?	**COURTESY**	Be prompt and generous when anyone asks you for your help. Better yet, do it before someone asks you.	Not recognizing the inherent dignity of others made in God's image and likeness

PLAN FOR LENT

Prudence

Prudence all the virtues and enables us to judge rightly how we should act in a given situation. After reflecting on the three forms of penance, you are ready to make a "fitness plan" for your heart. Consider each form of penance. Where is God calling you to grow this Lent?

By following the three parts of a prudential act, you will be able to prudently discern how your days of Lent will be observed. This plan will be an intellectual decision that will help you to courageously undertake and persevere in good works until the glorious solemnity of Easter.

		Notes
Good Counsel (Ask and Listen)	Prayerfully examine how you can cultivate particular virtues. If necessary, ask a parent or trustworthy friend for a suggestion.	
Good Judgment (Think)	Think and pray about what you should do to condition your heart.	
Command (Act)	Make a decision to do it!	

PLAN FOR LENT

Choose a specific area for each type of penance where you want to grow in virtue. In the space provided, write down the virtue you wish to cultivate and your plan for cultivating that virtue.

Complete the chart to identify your "fitness plan" for Lent.

Form of penance	Virtue to cultivate	Ways to cultivate
Fasting		
Prayer		
Almsgiving		

OR

Select one or more virtues from the Disciple of Christ Virtue Chart (see pp. 22 & 23).

Virtue to cultivate	Ways to cultivate

PLAN FOR LENT

Fortitude is the cardinal virtue that enables one to endure difficulties and pain for the sake of what is good. Therefore, pray for an increase of fortitude and the grace to persevere.

Prayer for Perseverance:

Below write your own prayer, asking God for the grace of perseverance in your Lenten resolutions:

_____
_____
_____

Courtesy of Debbie Herbeck

DISCIPLE OF CHRIST VIRTUES

IN BAPTISM WE ARE GRAFTED ONTO CHRIST THE VINE; He enters us and remains in us as long as we desire His presence. By freely choosing to live as one with Christ, we permit Him to transform us from within. This life in Christ is rooted in the virtues and gifts received at baptism (see *CCC*, 1266).

"If faith is like the root, charity is like the sap that nourishes the trunk and rises into the branches, the network of virtues, to produce the delicious fruit of good works" (Servais Pinckaers, O.P., *Morality: The Catholic View*, South Bend, St. Augustine Press, 2001).

Disciple of Christ Virtues guide educators, parents, and students in identifying virtues which need to be cultivated. Each corresponding "Opposing Trait" highlights a pattern of behavior which needs change in order for one to mature in virtue.

Human virtues acquired by education, by deliberate acts, and by perseverance ever-renewed in repeated efforts are purified and elevated by divine grace. With God's help, they forge character and give facility in the practice of the good. The virtuous man is happy to practice them (CCC, 1810).

"GOD GIVES THE GROWTH."
(1 CORINTHIANS 3:7)

VIRTUE	MEANING	OPPOSING TRAIT	WAYS TO CULTIVATE
JUSTICE (Fairness)	Enables one to give to each, beginning with God, what is due him	Failing to see what is owed to each by virtue of his dignity	Recognize what is due to God first and then to others.
AFFABILITY	Being easy to approach and easy to talk to — friendly	Being mean, unkind, cruel, or unflattering	Smile: acknowledge the presence of other people and take time to listen to them.
COURTESY	Treating other people with respect, recognizing that all are made in God's image and likeness	Not recognizing the inherent dignity of others made in God's image and likeness	Be aware of others' feelings and expressions; be polite, well-mannered.
GENEROSITY	Giving of oneself in a willing and cheerful manner for the good of others	Giving without a spirit of cheer, with a begrudging manner	Be self-giving; focus on one act of charity/kindness each day; share.
GRATITUDE	Thankful disposition of mind and heart	Not expressing appreciation; taking other people and things for granted	Count the good things (blessings) in one's life; express gratitude even when it is difficult.
KINDNESS	Expressing genuine concern about the well-being of others; anticipating their needs	Not regarding the well-being of others, being cruel in looks, words, and actions	Practice speaking, thinking, and acting kindly.
LOYALTY	Accepting the bonds implicit in relationships and defending the virtues upheld by Church, family, and country	Breaking bonds of trust with Church, family, country, friends, and school	Seek to do one's best to help others; follow rules; fulfill responsibilities; be faithful to commitments.
OBEDIENCE	Assenting to rightful authority without hesitation or resistance	Resisting the directives of rightful authority	Listen to rightful authority; follow directions; give a prompt response.
PATRIOTISM	Paying due honor and respect to one's country, with a willingness to serve	Lacking regard or respect for one's country and national symbols	Show respect for your country's flag; speak respectfully about government officials; recite the Pledge.
PRAYERFULNESS	Being still, listening, and being willing to talk to God as a friend	Entertaining distractions during prayers and Mass	Cultivate a spirit of prayer and recollection; maintain the proper posture (kneeling, sitting still, etc.).
RESPECT	Speaking and acting according to one's own and others' rights, status, and circumstances	Resisting the directives of rightful authority	Be respectful in words and actions (body language); allow others to go first.
RESPONSIBILITY	Fulfilling one's just duties; accepting the consequences of one's words and actions, intentional and unintentional	Failing to accept responsibility for one's words and/or actions; being unreliable	Be accountable for one's personal actions and decisions at home, at school, and in personal relationships.
SINCERITY	Trustfulness in words and actions; honesty and enthusiasm towards others	Speaking or acting in a manner only to make oneself look good; being insincere	Tell the whole truth; build trust by words and actions; state what one is sorry for.
TRUSTWORTHINESS	Acting in a way that inspires confidence and trust; being reliable	Being devious or deceptive	Perform actions that restore and maintain trust; act with fidelity in small matters.

VIRTUE	MEANING	OPPOSING TRAIT	WAYS TO CULTIVATE
PRUDENCE (Sound Judgment)	Enables one to reason and to act rightly in any given situation — "right reason in action"	Being hasty or rash in one's words or actions	Pray for guidance. Seek sound advice. Think about the situation. Act upon the decision.
PARTS OF A PRUDENTIAL ACT			
GOOD COUNSEL (Ask and listen)	Seeking advice from a reasonable person	Seeking advice from those who agree with you; asking moral advice from people who do not share your moral values	Seek advice from trustworthy people.
GOOD JUDGMENT (Think)	Thinking rightly about a decision	Acting without thinking	Carefully consider all the circumstances and ask "What am I to do now?"
COMMAND (Act)	Directly acting upon a sound decision	Failing to act upon a sound decision	Take action after thoughtful deliberation.
VIRTUES			
CIRCUMSPECTION	Careful consideration of circumstances and consequences	Considering only oneself when acting	Seek advice silently reflect upon the circumstances and consequences of one's actions (memory).
DOCILITY	Willingness to be taught	Being stubborn, inflexible, and proudly set in one's ways	Listen to others and be willing to follow directions; thank others for rightful corrections.
FORESIGHT	Consideration of the consequences of one's actions; thinking ahead	Failing to consider later consequences	Pray, think, act; learn how to gather information to make a decision; plan out long-term and short-term goals.

VIRTUE	MEANING	OPPOSING TRAIT	WAYS TO CULTIVATE
FORTITUDE (Courage)	Enables one to endure difficulties and pain for the sake of what is good	Choosing the easiest task; being cowardly; being insensible to fear	Withstand difficulties; complete hard tasks.
INDUSTRIOUSNESS	Diligence, especially in work that leads to natural and supernatural maturity	Giving in to a lack of motivation to complete one's responsibilities; being lazy	Diligently complete a task; set small goals along the way.
MAGNANIMITY	Seeking with confidence to do great things in God; literally "having a large soul"	Seeking to do great things for self-promotion — not seeking to do the good that is possible — pusillanimity (weak, spineless)	Acknowledge the good in others when it is difficult; strive to do difficult tasks with God's grace.
MAGNIFICENCE	Doing great things for God	Being wasteful; not responding to grace	Use one's talents for the good; act with generosity towards others.
PATIENCE	Bearing present difficulties calmly	Being impatient while completing a difficult task or in handling challenging circumstances	Listen to others; wait for one's turn; tolerate inconveniences and annoyances without complaining.
PERSEVERANCE	Taking the steps necessary to carry out objectives in spite of difficulties	Quickly giving up when a task is challenging	Complete task from start to finish; stay with a task when it is hard, difficult, or boring.

VIRTUE	MEANING	OPPOSING TRAIT	WAYS TO CULTIVATE
TEMPERANCE (Self-Control)	Enables one to be moderate in the pleasure and use of created goods	Intemperance; overindulging in a good thing	Exercise the freedom to say "no" to one's wants and desires.
HONESTY	Sincerity, openness and truthfulness in one's words and actions	Being dishonest in words and actions; telling lies	Live uprightly in words and actions; recognize that "God sees the heart."
HUMILITY	Awareness that all one's gifts come from God and appreciation for the gifts of others	Failing to recognize the gifts of others; being too proud or having false humility	Show deference to others; acknowledge the accomplishments of others; look at one's strengths and weaknesses honestly.
MEEKNESS	Serenity of spirit while focusing on the needs of others	Giving in to anger and losing one's temper when working or playing with others	Remain calm; allow others to go first; wait without complaining.
MODERATION	Attention to balance in one's life	Giving in to being excessive in one or more areas of one's life	Set limits for oneself; create a balance in one's life by limiting the use of media, consumption of additional food and drink, etc.
MODESTY	Purity of heart in action, especially in regards to dress and speech	Choosing to dress or act in a way inconsistent with one's dignity as a child of God	Follow the dress code; recognize your dignity as a person; ask yourself if you are respecting yourself as a child of God.
ORDERLINESS	Keeping oneself physically clean and neat and one's belongings in good order	Disorder with regard to one's space and physical appearance	Establish order in one's daily life; keep one's space and appearance orderly and clean.
SELF-CONTROL	Joyful mastery over one's passions and desires	Being excessive in words or actions, acting impulsively	Mastery of one's desires; practice restraint in regards to words and actions.

LECTIO DIVINA

Living Lent with the Word

"Meditation engages thought, imagination, emotion, and desire. This mobilization of faculties is necessary in order to deepen our convictions of faith, prompt the conversion of our hearts, and strengthen our will to follow Christ." (CCC, 2708)

As you open your mind and heart to the Holy Spirit and encounter the Word of God, you will begin to experience a renewed faith and a closer relationship with the person of Jesus Christ. The questions are written to guide your prayerful reading of Scripture and assist you in understanding the passage. They are not intended to be questions to complete for an assignment but more of a means for you to establish a relationship with Jesus.

- In a spirit of recollection, place yourself in God's presence.

- Recite the prayer: *Lord Jesus Christ, Son of the Living God, have mercy on me, a sinner.*

- Daily read the Scripture verses and follow the steps for Lectio Divina. Let the Word of God penetrate your mind and heart, and ponder the Word throughout the course of the day.

The Mocking of Christ with the Virgin and St. Dominic by Fra Angelico © Church of San Marco, Florence, Italy / The Bridgeman Art Library

GRATITUDE LOG

While the Lenten season can seem somber as we focus on living and practicing the forms of penance, it is important to keep our hearts centered on Easter and God's love for us. It is easy to quickly fall into a spirit of negativity and only see the mistakes we have made. Therefore, it is essential to keep before us God's goodness and love, which springs from a grateful heart.

Make an effort each day to write about a situation that made you happy and give praise to God.

Psalm 150

Hallelujah!

Praise God in his holy sanctuary;
give praise in the mighty dome of heaven.

Give praise for his mighty deeds,
praise him for his great majesty.

Give praise with blasts upon the horn,
praise him with harp and lyre.

Give praise with tambourines and dance,
praise him with strings and pipes.

Give praise with crashing cymbals,
praise him with sounding cymbals.

Let everything that has breath
give praise to the LORD!

Hallelujah!

The Last Judgement, Angelico, Fra (Guido di Pietro) / Museo di San Marco dell'Angelico, Florence, Italy / The Bridgeman Art Library Workbook

FEBRUARY 18 — ASH WEDNESDAY

MATTHEW 6:1–6, 16–18

Jesus said to his disciples: "Take care not to perform righteous deeds in order that people may see them; otherwise, you will have recompense from your heavenly Father. When you give alms, do not blow a trumpet before you, as the hypocrites do in the synagogues and in the streets to win the praise of others. Amen, I say to you, they have received their reward. But when you give alms, do not let your left hand know what your right is doing, so that your almsgiving may be secret. And your Father who sees in secret will repay you.

"When you pray, do not be like the hypocrites, who love to stand and pray in the synagogues and on street corners so that others may see them. Amen, I say to you, they have received their reward. But when you pray, go to your inner room, close the door, and pray to your Father in secret. And your Father who sees in secret will repay you.

"When you fast, do not look gloomy like the hypocrites. They neglect their appearance, so that they may appear to others to be fasting. Amen, I say to you, they have received their reward. But when you fast, anoint your head and wash your face, so that you may not appear to be fasting, except to your Father who is hidden. And your Father who sees what is hidden will repay you."

God's Word strikes the heart. What word or phrase struck your heart?

_____
_____
_____
_____
_____

What does Jesus teach about:

Giving alms: _____

Praying: _____

Fasting: _____

FEBRUARY 18 — ASH WEDNESDAY (CONTINUED)

"Jesus, You taught us that our Father sees the heart. Show me where I can 'blow the trumpet,' standing so others may see me looking gloomy." Write down ways you need to change.

_____
_____
_____

With gratitude I praise You, God, for:

_____
_____

FEBRUARY 19 — THURSDAY AFTER ASH WEDNESDAY

LUKE 9:22-25

Jesus said to his disciples: "The Son of Man must suffer greatly and be rejected by the elders, the chief priests, and the scribes, and be killed and on the third day be raised."

Then he said to all, "If anyone wishes to come after me, he must deny himself and take up his cross daily and follow me. For whoever wishes to save his life will lose it, but whoever loses his life for my sake will save it. What profit is there for one to gain the whole world yet lose or forfeit himself?"

God's Word strikes the heart. What word or phrase struck your heart?

_____
_____

Jesus warns His disciples about His future suffering. How would this knowledge give them hope when the Son of Man suffers greatly?

_____
_____
_____

Jesus tells us to follow Him means to carry the cross daily. How does the theological virtue of hope strengthen us to endure our daily crosses?

_____
_____

It is hard to deny ourselves. Ask Jesus this question in prayer: "In what ways can I better carry my crosses? How can I die to self in order to bear the cross?"

_____
_____

With gratitude I praise You, God, for:

_____
_____

FEBRUARY 20 — FRIDAY AFTER ASH WEDNESDAY

MATTHEW 9:14–15

The disciples of John approached Jesus and said, "Why do we and the Pharisees fast much, but your disciples do not fast?" Jesus answered them, "Can the wedding guests mourn as long as the bridegroom is with them? The days will come when the bridegroom is taken away from them, and then they will fast."

God's Word strikes the heart. What word or phrase struck your heart?

_____
_____

What is the purpose of fasting? (See page 12.)

_____
_____
_____

Ask Jesus this question in prayer: "Jesus, show me an area in my life where Your presence is needed. How can fasting prepare me to receive You?" Write down what you hear Him say to you.

_____
_____
_____

With gratitude I praise You, God, for:

_____
_____

FEBRUARY 21 — SATURDAY AFTER ASH WEDNESDAY

LUKE 5:27–32

Jesus saw a tax collector named Levi sitting at the customs post. He said to him, "Follow me." And leaving everything behind, he got up and followed him. Then Levi gave a great banquet for him in his house, and a large crowd of tax collectors and others were at table with them. The Pharisees and their scribes complained to his disciples, saying, "Why do you eat and drink with tax collectors and sinners?" Jesus said to them in reply, "Those who are healthy do not need a physician, but the sick do. I have not come to call the righteous to repentance but sinners."

God's Word strikes the heart. What word or phrase struck your heart?

What is unusual about Jesus calling Matthew (Levi) to follow Him?

Jesus entered the house of Matthew and ate with his friends — other tax collectors. How did the Pharisees react?

Ask this question in prayer: "Jesus, do I judge others by their external actions? How are You showing me to not judge others?" Write down what you hear Him saying to you.

With gratitude I praise You, God, for:

FEBRUARY 22 — FIRST SUNDAY OF LENT

MARK 1:12-15

The Spirit drove Jesus out into the desert, and he remained in the desert for forty days, tempted by Satan. He was among wild beasts, and the angels ministered to him.

After John had been arrested, Jesus came to Galilee proclaiming the gospel of God: "This is the time of fulfillment. The kingdom of God is at hand. Repent, and believe in the gospel."

God's Word strikes the heart. What word or phrase struck your heart?

_____
_____
_____

Describe Jesus' experience in the desert.

_____
_____
_____
_____

Often you are tempted just like Jesus. Who can you pray to when you are encountering Satan?

_____
_____
_____

Ask this question in prayer: "Jesus, show me the occasion of temptations which prevent me from repenting and believing in the gospel." Write down what He says to you.

_____
_____
_____
_____

With gratitude I praise You, God, for:

_____
_____
_____

FEBRUARY 23 — MONDAY OF THE FIRST WEEK OF LENT

MATTHEW 25:31-46

Jesus said to his disciples: "When the Son of Man comes in his glory, and all the angels with him, he will sit upon his glorious throne, and all the nations will be assembled before him. And he will separate them one from another, as a shepherd separates the sheep from the goats. He will place the sheep on his right and the goats on his left. Then the king will say to those on his right, 'Come, you who are blessed by my Father. Inherit the kingdom prepared for you from the foundation of the world. For I was hungry and you gave me food, I was thirsty and you gave me drink, a stranger and you welcomed me, naked and you clothed me, ill and you cared for me, in prison and you visited me.' Then the righteous will answer him and say, 'Lord, when did we see you hungry and feed you, or thirsty and give you drink? When did we see you a stranger and welcome you, or naked and clothe you? When did we see you ill or in prison, and visit you?' And the king will say to them in reply, 'Amen, I say to you, whatever you did for one of these least brothers of mine, you did for me.' Then he will say to those on his left, 'Depart from me, you accursed, into the eternal fire prepared for the Devil and his angels. For I was hungry and you gave me no food, I was thirsty and you gave me no drink, a stranger and you gave me no welcome, naked and you gave me no clothing, ill and in prison, and you did not care for me.' Then they will answer and say, 'Lord, when did we see you hungry or thirsty or a stranger or naked or ill or in prison, and not minister to your needs?' He will answer them, 'Amen, I say to you, what you did not do for one of these least ones, you did not do for me.' And these will go off to eternal punishment, but the righteous to eternal life."

God's Word strikes the heart. What word or phrase struck your heart?

_____
_____

Describe the virtues possessed by the sheep.

_____
_____
_____

Describe the vices possessed by the goats.

_____
_____
_____

FEBRUARY 23 — MONDAY OF THE FIRST WEEK OF LENT

Examine your own life. How do you:

Give to the hungry? _____

Give drink to the thirsty? _____

Welcome a stranger? _____

Clothe those in need? _____

Care for the sick? _____

Visit those imprisoned? _____

Ask this question in prayer: "Jesus, it is easy to become selfish and think only of my wants. Help me to be more generous toward the least ones. Show me one way I can change." Write down what you hear Him say to you.

_____
_____
_____

With gratitude I praise You, God, for:

_____
_____

FEBRUARY 24 — TUESDAY OF THE FIRST WEEK OF LENT

MATTHEW 6:7–15

Jesus said to his disciples: "In praying, do not babble like the pagans, who think that they will be heard because of their many words. Do not be like them. Your Father knows what you need before you ask him.

"This is how you are to pray:

Our Father who art in heaven,
hallowed be thy name,
thy Kingdom come
thy will be done,
on earth as it is in heaven.
Give us this day our daily bread
and forgive us our trespasses,
as we forgive those who trespass against us;
and lead us not into temptation,
but deliver us from evil.

"If you forgive men their transgressions, your heavenly Father will forgive you. But if you do not forgive men, neither will your Father forgive your transgressions."

God's Word strikes the heart. What word or phrase struck your heart?

_____
_____
_____

What is your favorite line of the Our Father? Why?

_____
_____
_____

 To forgive is difficult if the other person has not expressed remorse or an apology. Ask yourself if you have failed to humbly apologize to someone. If so, pray for that person and find an occasion to express your apology.

FEBRUARY 24 — TUESDAY OF THE FIRST WEEK OF LENT (CONTINUED)

Jesus, our merciful Savior, gives us grace to forgive those who transgress against us. To nurse a grudge keeps us from living freely. Ask Jesus to free your heart from a grudge. Write down what He says to you.

_____
_____
_____

The disciples asked Jesus to teach them how to pray. This painting shows Mary teaching Jesus how to pray. What do you think He learned from His mother? In what ways do you think Mary taught Jesus to pray?

_____
_____
_____
_____
_____
_____

How can you cultivate the virtue of prayerfulness?

_____
_____
_____
_____
_____
_____

Virgin of the Ghiara (Madonna della Ghiara) by Ludovico Lana / Mondadori Portfolio/Electa/Nuova Alfa Editoriale / Bridgeman Images

With gratitude I praise You, God, for:

_____
_____

FEBRUARY 25 — WEDNESDAY OF THE FIRST WEEK OF LENT

LUKE 11:29–32

While still more people gathered in the crowd, Jesus said to them, "This generation is an evil generation; it seeks a sign, but no sign will be given it, except the sign of Jonah. Just as Jonah became a sign to the Ninevites, so will the Son of Man be to this generation. At the judgment the queen of the south will rise with the men of this generation and she will condemn them, because she came from the ends of the earth to hear the wisdom of Solomon, and there is something greater than Solomon here. At the judgment the men of Nineveh will arise with this generation and condemn it, because at the preaching of Jonah they repented, and there is something greater than Jonah here."

God's Word strikes the heart. What word or phrase struck your heart?

___

Recall the Old Testament story of Jonah and how he led the Ninevites to prayer and penance. Jesus is the Son of Man. How is He a sign to this generation?

___

What virtues are necessary for a person to be able to hear teachings and preaching about Jesus?

___

Ask the Holy Spirit, who is the Spirit of Truth, to open your heart so you may hear God's Word. Write down one distraction you experience in prayer.

___

With gratitude I praise You, God, for:

___

FEBRUARY 26 — THURSDAY OF THE FIRST WEEK OF LENT

MATTHEW 7:7-12

Jesus said to his disciples: "Ask and it will be given to you; seek and you will find; knock and the door will be opened to you. For everyone who asks, receives; and the one who seeks, finds; and to the one who knocks, the door will be opened. Which one of you would hand his son a stone when he asked for a loaf of bread, or a snake when he asked for a fish? If you then, who are wicked, know how to give good gifts to your children, how much more will your heavenly Father give good things to those who ask him.

"Do to others whatever you would have them do to you. This is the law and the prophets."

There are usually four ways God responds to our prayers:

1. **Slow** — God teaches us to persevere in prayer and wait for an answer.
2. **Grow** — God delays His answer to expand and prepare our hearts.
3. **No** — God, in His providential care, knows our prayer is not accordance with His loving will.
4. **Go** — God answers our prayer.

God's Word strikes the heart. What word or phrase struck your heart?

_____
_____

John was present when Jesus taught the disciples about prayers of petition. He would later write, "Beloved: we have this confidence in him that if we ask anything according to his will, he hears us" (1 John 5:14). What does this teach you about prayer?

_____
_____

Ask this question in prayer: "Jesus, You lived each moment in obedience to Your heavenly Father's will. How can I learn to trust Him and believe He will not give me a stone instead of bread?" Listen in silence and write about a time He answered your prayers.

_____
_____
_____

✝ With gratitude I praise You, God, for:

_____

FEBRUARY 27 — FRIDAY OF THE FIRST WEEK OF LENT

MATTHEW 5:20-26

Jesus said to his disciples: "I tell you, unless your righteousness surpasses that of the scribes and Pharisees, you will not enter into the Kingdom of heaven.

"You have heard that it was said to your ancestors, You shall not kill; and whoever kills will be liable to judgment. But I say to you, whoever is angry with his brother will be liable to judgment, and whoever says to his brother, Raqa, will be answerable to the Sanhedrin, and whoever says, 'You fool,' will be liable to fiery Gehenna. Therefore, if you bring your gift to the altar, and there recall that your brother has anything against you, leave your gift there at the altar, go first and be reconciled with your brother, and then come and offer your gift. Settle with your opponent quickly while on the way to court. Otherwise your opponent will hand you over to the judge, and the judge will hand you over to the guard, and you will be thrown into prison. Amen, I say to you, you will not be released until you have paid the last penny."

God's Word strikes the heart. What word or phrase struck your heart?

_____

_____

Justice enables one to give to each, beginning with God, what is due to him. How does Jesus challenge His disciples to live justly?

_____

_____

What virtues are necessary for one to live righteously? Describe how this is different than the scribes and Pharisees.

_____

_____

Sometimes people are unwilling to accept our apology or forgiveness. Ask Jesus to teach you how to reconcile with those who refuse to be reconciled. Write a prayer which reflects His message to you.

_____

_____

With gratitude I praise You, God, for:

_____

FEBRUARY 28 — SATURDAY OF THE FIRST WEEK OF LENT

MATTHEW 5:43-48

Jesus said to his disciples: "You have heard that it was said, You shall love your neighbor and hate your enemy. But I say to you, love your enemies, and pray for those who persecute you, that you may be children of your heavenly Father, for he makes his sun rise on the bad and the good, and causes rain to fall on the just and the unjust. For if you love those who love you, what recompense will you have? Do not the tax collectors do the same? And if you greet your brothers and sisters only, what is unusual about that? Do not the pagans do the same? So be perfect, just as your heavenly Father is perfect."

God's Word strikes the heart. What word or phrase struck your heart?

_____
_____

"He makes his sun rise on the bad and the good, and causes rain to fall on the just and the unjust." What does Jesus mean in this statement?

_____
_____
_____

How are we called to love our enemies?

_____
_____
_____

Write a prayer asking Jesus to give you His love so you can love those who are not friendly or who have persecuted you.

_____
_____
_____

With gratitude I praise You, God, for:

_____
_____

MARCH 1 — SECOND SUNDAY OF LENT

MARK 9:2-10

Jesus took Peter, James, and John and led them up a high mountain apart by themselves. And he was transfigured before them, and his clothes became dazzling white, such as no fuller on earth could bleach them. Then Elijah appeared to them along with Moses, and they were conversing with Jesus. Then Peter said to Jesus in reply, "Rabbi, it is good that we are here! Let us make three tents: one for you, one for Moses, and one for Elijah." He hardly knew what to say, they were so terrified. Then a cloud came, casting a shadow over them; from the cloud came a voice, "This is my beloved Son. Listen to him." Suddenly, looking around, they no longer saw anyone but Jesus alone with them.

As they were coming down from the mountain, he charged them not to relate what they had seen to anyone, except when the Son of Man had risen from the dead. So they kept the matter to themselves, questioning what rising from the dead meant.

God's Word strikes the heart. What word or phrase struck your heart?

_____
_____

Who appeared to the apostles with Jesus? What was said from the cloud?

_____
_____

Which person of the Trinity is manifested in each of the following:

Voice speaking _____

Transfigured _____

Cloud overshadowing _____

Ask this question in prayer: "Jesus, You were transfigured before Your apostles and revealed Yourself in glory. How can this truth strengthen me during difficult times?" Write down what you hear Him saying to you.

_____
_____

With gratitude I praise You, God, for:

_____

MARCH 2 — MONDAY OF THE SECOND WEEK OF LENT

LUKE 6:36–38

Jesus said to his disciples: "Be merciful, just as your Father is merciful.

"Stop judging and you will not be judged. Stop condemning and you will not be condemned. Forgive and you will be forgiven. Give and gifts will be given to you; a good measure, packed together, shaken down, and overflowing, will be poured into your lap. For the measure with which you measure will in return be measured out to you."

God's Word strikes the heart. What word or phrase struck your heart?

___

Think of a time you have been judged by another person. Were you hurt or upset? Why or why not?

___

Think of a time you have judged or condemned others. How did you feel? Were you hurt?

___

"Jesus, You revealed to us the merciful heart of Your heavenly Father. Show me when I am quick to judge others so I may change." Write down what He says to you.

___

With gratitude I praise You, God, for:

___

MARCH 3 — TUESDAY OF THE SECOND WEEK OF LENT

MATTHEW 23:1-12

Jesus spoke to the crowds and to his disciples, saying, "The scribes and the Pharisees have taken their seat on the chair of Moses. Therefore, do and observe all things whatsoever they tell you, but do not follow their example. For they preach but they do not practice. They tie up heavy burdens hard to carry and lay them on people's shoulders, but they will not lift a finger to move them. All their works are performed to be seen. They widen their phylacteries and lengthen their tassels. They love places of honor at banquets, seats of honor in synagogues, greetings in marketplaces, and the salutation 'Rabbi.' As for you, do not be called 'Rabbi.' You have but one teacher, and you are all brothers. Call no one on earth your father; you have but one Father in heaven. Do not be called 'Master'; you have but one master, the Christ. The greatest among you must be your servant. Whoever exalts himself will be humbled; but whoever humbles himself will be exalted."

God's Word strikes the heart. What word or phrase struck your heart?

_____
_____

How do you feel when someone says one thing but does the opposite?

_____
_____

Jesus boldly speaks about the hypocrisy of scribes and Pharisees. How is humility the solution to "exalting ourselves"? What other virtues should you seek to practice?

_____
_____

Ask this question in prayer: "Jesus, meek and humble of heart, how do I exalt myself or fail to live what I preach to others?" Write down what He says to you.

_____
_____

With gratitude I praise You, God, for:

_____
_____

Jesus, meek and humble of heart, make my heart like unto Thine.

MARCH 4 — WEDNESDAY OF THE SECOND WEEK OF LENT

MATTHEW 20:17-28

As Jesus was going up to Jerusalem, he took the Twelve disciples aside by themselves, and said to them on the way, "Behold, we are going up to Jerusalem, and the Son of Man will be handed over to the chief priests and the scribes, and they will condemn him to death, and hand him over to the Gentiles to be mocked and scourged and crucified, and he will be raised on the third day."

Then the mother of the sons of Zebedee approached Jesus with her sons and did him homage, wishing to ask him for something. He said to her, "What do you wish?" She answered him, "Command that these two sons of mine sit, one at your right and the other at your left, in your kingdom." Jesus said in reply, "You do not know what you are asking. Can you drink the chalice that I am going to drink?" They said to him, "We can." He replied, "My chalice you will indeed drink, but to sit at my right and at my left, this is not mine to give but is for those for whom it has been prepared by my Father." When the ten heard this, they became indignant at the two brothers. But Jesus summoned them and said, "You know that the rulers of the Gentiles lord it over them, and the great ones make their authority over them felt. But it shall not be so among you. Rather, whoever wishes to be great among you shall be your servant; whoever wishes to be first among you shall be your slave. Just so, the Son of Man did not come to be served but to serve and to give his life as a ransom for many."

God's Word strikes the heart. What word or phrase struck your heart?

_____

_____

How do you think the disciples felt when Jesus predicted His death and resurrection?

_____

_____

_____

When Jesus replied to the mother of the sons of Zebedee, "You do not know what you are asking," what do you think He meant?

_____

_____

_____

MARCH 4 — WEDNESDAY OF THE SECOND WEEK OF LENT (CONTINUED)

Jesus said, "The Son of Man did not come to be served but to serve and to give his life as a ransom for many." How did Jesus serve and give His life as a ransom?

_____
_____
_____

Ask this question in prayer: "Jesus, at times it is hard to serve others. How can I better serve others?" Write down what He says to you.

_____
_____
_____

With gratitude I praise You, God, for:

_____
_____

✝ Lenten Check Point

Out of love, Jesus took His disciples aside and told them about His future suffering, crucifixion, and resurrection. During Lent our penance helps us to prepare for the times we are asked to join with Christ and carry our cross. Spend a few moments reflecting upon your Lenten journey and write your thoughts.

_____
_____
_____
_____

MARCH 5 — THURSDAY OF THE SECOND WEEK OF LENT

LUKE 16:19-3

Jesus said to the Pharisees: "There was a rich man who dressed in purple garments and fine linen and dined sumptuously each day. And lying at his door was a poor man named Lazarus, covered with sores, who would gladly have eaten his fill of the scraps that fell from the rich man's table. Dogs even used to come and lick his sores. When the poor man died, he was carried away by angels to the bosom of Abraham. The rich man also died and was buried, and from the netherworld, where he was in torment, he raised his eyes and saw Abraham far off and Lazarus at his side. And he cried out, 'Father Abraham, have pity on me. Send Lazarus to dip the tip of his finger in water and cool my tongue, for I am suffering torment in these flames.' Abraham replied, 'My child, remember that you received what was good during your lifetime while Lazarus likewise received what was bad; but now he is comforted here, whereas you are tormented. Moreover, between us and you a great chasm is established to prevent anyone from crossing who might wish to go from our side to yours or from your side to ours.' He said, 'Then I beg you, father, send him to my father's house, for I have five brothers, so that he may warn them, lest they too come to this place of torment.' But Abraham replied, 'They have Moses and the prophets. Let them listen to them.' He said, 'Oh no, father Abraham, but if someone from the dead goes to them, they will repent.' Then Abraham said, 'If they will not listen to Moses and the prophets, neither will they be persuaded if someone should rise from the dead.'"

God's Word strikes the heart. What word or phrase struck your heart?

_____

_____

Compare the rich man and Lazarus before their death and afterward.

	Before Death	After Death
Rich Man		
Lazarus		

MARCH 5 — THURSDAY OF THE SECOND WEEK OF LENT (CONTINUED)

The Rich Man in Hell, illustration for *The Life of Christ*, Tissot, James Jacques Joseph / Brooklyn Museum of Art, New York, USA / Bridgeman Images

What is the great chasm?

_____
_____
_____
_____

Dullness of sense is a weak mental vision of spiritual goods. How does sin prevent the five brothers from listening to Moses and the prophets?

_____
_____
_____
_____
_____
_____

Jesus, you taught us, "Blessed are the poor in spirit, for theirs is the kingdom of heaven" (Matthew 5:2). Ask Jesus this question in prayer: "In what ways do I treasure the things of this world as opposed to laying up treasures in heaven" (See Matthew 6:19–21). Write down what He says to you.

_____
_____
_____
_____
_____
_____

✝ With gratitude I praise You, God, for:

_____
_____
_____

MARCH 6 — FRIDAY OF THE SECOND WEEK OF LENT

MATTHEW 21:33-43, 45-46

Jesus said to the chief priests and the elders of the people: "Hear another parable. There was a landowner who planted a vineyard, put a hedge around it, dug a wine press in it, and built a tower. Then he leased it to tenants and went on a journey. When vintage time drew near, he sent his servants to the tenants to obtain his produce. But the tenants seized the servants and one they beat, another they killed, and a third they stoned. Again he sent other servants, more numerous than the first ones, but they treated them in the same way. Finally, he sent his son to them, thinking, 'They will respect my son.' But when the tenants saw the son, they said to one another, 'This is the heir. Come, let us kill him and acquire his inheritance.' They seized him, threw him out of the vineyard, and killed him. What will the owner of the vineyard do to those tenants when he comes?" They answered him, "He will put those wretched men to a wretched death and lease his vineyard to other tenants who will give him the produce at the proper times." Jesus said to them, "Did you never read in the Scriptures:

*The stone that the builders rejected
has become the cornerstone;
by the Lord has this been done,
and it is wonderful in our eyes?*

Therefore, I say to you, the Kingdom of God will be taken away from you and given to a people that will produce its fruit." When the chief priests and the Pharisees heard his parables, they knew that he was speaking about them. And although they were attempting to arrest him, they feared the crowds, for they regarded him as a prophet.

God's Word strikes the heart. What word or phrase struck your heart?

_____
_____
_____

The land owner entrusted his vineyard to other tenants. What happened to his vineyard?

_____
_____
_____

How is Jesus the cornerstone of your soul?

_____
_____
_____

With gratitude I praise You, God, for:

_____
_____

MARCH 7 — SATURDAY OF THE SECOND WEEK OF LENT

LUKE 15:1-3, 11–32

Tax collectors and sinners were all drawing near to listen to Jesus, but the Pharisees and scribes began to complain, saying, "This man welcomes sinners and eats with them." So to them Jesus addressed this parable. "A man had two sons, and the younger son said to his father, 'Father, give me the share of your estate that should come to me.' So the father divided the property between them. After a few days, the younger son collected all his belongings and set off to a distant country where he squandered his inheritance on a life of dissipation. When he had freely spent everything, a severe famine struck that country, and he found himself in dire need. So he hired himself out to one of the local citizens who sent him to his farm to tend the swine. And he longed to eat his fill of the pods on which the swine fed, but nobody gave him any. Coming to his senses he thought, 'How many of my father's hired workers have more than enough food to eat, but here am I, dying from hunger. I shall get up and go to my father and I shall say to him, "Father, I have sinned against heaven and against you. I no longer deserve to be called your son; treat me as you would treat one of your hired workers."' So he got up and went back to his father. While he was still a long way off, his father caught sight of him, and was filled with compassion. He ran to his son, embraced him and kissed him. His son said to him, 'Father, I have sinned against heaven and against you; I no longer deserve to be called your son.' But his father ordered his servants, 'Quickly, bring the finest robe and put it on him; put a ring on his finger and sandals on his feet. Take the fattened calf and slaughter it. Then let us celebrate with a feast, because this son of mine was dead, and has come to life again; he was lost, and has been found.' Then the celebration began. Now the older son had been out in the field and, on his way back, as he neared the house, he heard the sound of music and dancing. He called one of the servants and asked what this might mean. The servant said to him, 'Your brother has returned and your father has slaughtered the fattened calf because he has him back safe and sound.' He became angry, and when he refused to enter the house, his father came out and pleaded with him. He said to his father in reply, 'Look, all these years I served you and not once did I disobey your orders; yet you never gave me even a young goat to feast on with my friends. But when your son returns who swallowed up your property with prostitutes, for him you slaughter the fattened calf.' He said to him, 'My son, you are here with me always; everything I have is yours. But now we must celebrate and rejoice, because your brother was dead and has come to life again; he was lost and has been found.'"

God's Word strikes the heart. What word or phrase struck your heart?

_____

_____

_____

MARCH 7 — SATURDAY OF THE SECOND WEEK OF LENT (CONTINUED)

Why would there be more joy in heaven over the repentance of one sinner as opposed to ninety-nine righteous who have no need of repentance?

_____
_____
_____

Jesus speaks of the angels of God rejoicing over the repentance of one sinner. What does this teach you about God's love and mercy?

_____
_____
_____

With gratitude I praise You, God, for:

_____
_____
_____
_____
_____

Return of the Prodigal Son, 1773, Batoni, Pompeo Girolamo / Kunsthistorisches Museum, Vienna, Austria / Bridgeman Images

A letter from Audrey...

Lent 2015

Dear Disciple of Christ,

This Easter is my eight year anniversary as a Catholic. I can vividly remember my first Lent leading up to my confirmation and baptism: I was twenty-three years old. I had grown up, an Evangelical Protestant with no liturgical tradition—Lent with its stark sparseness and sobriety, leading up to the explosive spiritual springtime of Easter, was a rich and exciting experience for me that first time. Penance felt like a privilege! I felt so connected to Christ on the cross that year.

Since 2007, however, Lent has lost most of its novelty. I've grown "used to" the Church seasons. The honeymoon phase has ended, and now I find myself fighting yearly for some small bit of the fervor and passion I used to feel during the penitential season of Lent.

I'm telling you this because I suspect you're probably something like me. More than likely you're not totally happy with the way your Lenten journey is going. Perhaps you have slipped up on your penance a few times or forgotten to pray those extra decades you promised yourself you'd remember each night; or maybe you've been perfect about your penance, but it feels more like homework than a holy impulse. Maybe, like me, you just feel apathetic and unfocused most days during Lent, like you do most days during the year.

Here is a piece of beautiful news: Where we are faithless, God is faithful! I like to think that the Church set up the liturgical calendar because she knew we probably all needed quite a few Lents and Easters to learn how to receive the love of God into our cold hearts.

AUDREYASSAD.COM

If you're struggling this Lent, just take a breath, ask the Lord for His help, and begin again tomorrow. Lent is a journey, not a state of mind.

"Because of the Lord's great Love we are not consumed, for His compassions never fail. They are new every morning: great is Thy faithfulness." — Lamentations 3:22–23

Audrey Assad

MARCH 8 — THIRD SUNDAY OF LENT

JOHN 2:13–25

Since the Passover of the Jews was near, Jesus went up to Jerusalem. He found in the temple area those who sold oxen, sheep, and doves, as well as the money changers seated there. He made a whip out of cords and drove them all out of the temple area, with the sheep and oxen, and spilled the coins of the money changers and overturned their tables, and to those who sold doves he said, "Take these out of here, and stop making my Father's house a marketplace." His disciples recalled the words of Scripture, Zeal for your house will consume me. At this the Jews answered and said to him, "What sign can you show us for doing this?" Jesus answered and said to them, "Destroy this temple and in three days I will raise it up." The Jews said, "This temple has been under construction for forty-six years, and you will raise it up in three days?" But he was speaking about the temple of his body. Therefore, when he was raised from the dead, his disciples remembered that he had said this, and they came to believe the Scripture and the word Jesus had spoken.

While he was in Jerusalem for the feast of Passover, many began to believe in his name when they saw the signs he was doing. But Jesus would not trust himself to them because he knew them all, and did not need anyone to testify about human nature. He himself understood it well.

God's Word strikes the heart. What word or phrase struck your heart?

_____
_____

Describe Jesus' actions in the temple area. Why is His anger justified?

_____
_____

You are a temple of the Holy Spirit and redeemed by the blood of Jesus Christ. Imagine Jesus walking into the inner recesses of your heart. Ask Him in what ways your "temple area" needs to be overturned and renewed. Write down what you hear Him say.

_____
_____

With gratitude I praise You, God, for:

_____
_____

MARCH 9 — MONDAY OF THE THIRD WEEK OF LENT

LUKE 4:24–30

Jesus said to the people in the synagogue at Nazareth: "Amen, I say to you, no prophet is accepted in his own native place. Indeed, I tell you, there were many widows in Israel in the days of Elijah when the sky was closed for three and a half years and a severe famine spread over the entire land. It was to none of these that Elijah was sent, but only to a widow in Zarephath in the land of Sidon. Again, there were many lepers in Israel during the time of Elisha the prophet; yet not one of them was cleansed, but only Naaman the Syrian." When the people in the synagogue heard this, they were all filled with fury. They rose up, drove him out of the town, and led him to the brow of the hill on which their town had been built, to hurl him down headlong. But he passed through the midst of them and went away.

God's Word strikes the heart. What word or phrase struck your heart?

_____
_____

Jesus returns to his home town of Nazareth after traveling in the region of Capernaum. He enters the synagogue and reads from the scroll of the prophet Isaiah. How is this passage fulfilled in Jesus?

_____
_____

Why did the people of Nazareth reject Jesus' teaching? How did they react? How is their response different from those in Capernaum (see Mark 1:21–22)?

_____
_____

Ask Jesus this question in prayer: "Is there an area in my life where I am blind or held captive? Show me how I need to change." Write down what He says to you.

_____
_____

With gratitude I praise You, God, for:

_____
_____

MARCH 9 — MONDAY OF THE THIRD WEEK OF LENT (CONTINUED)

Christ Escapes the Pharisees, Overbeck, Friedrich / Koninklijk Museum voor Schone Kunsten, Antwerp, Belgium / © Lukas - Art in Flanders VZW / Photo: Hugo Maertens / Bridgeman Images

MARCH 10 — TUESDAY OF THE THIRD WEEK OF LENT

MATTHEW 18:21-35

Peter approached Jesus and asked him, "Lord, if my brother sins against me, how often must I forgive him? As many as seven times?" Jesus answered, "I say to you, not seven times but seventy-seven times. That is why the Kingdom of heaven may be likened to a king who decided to settle accounts with his servants. When he began the accounting, a debtor was brought before him who owed him a huge amount. Since he had no way of paying it back, his master ordered him to be sold, along with his wife, his children, and all his property, in payment of the debt. At that, the servant fell down, did him homage, and said, 'Be patient with me, and I will pay you back in full.' Moved with compassion the master of that servant let him go and forgave him the loan. When that servant had left, he found one of his fellow servants who owed him a much smaller amount. He seized him and started to choke him, demanding, 'Pay back what you owe.' Falling to his knees, his fellow servant begged him, 'Be patient with me, and I will pay you back.' But he refused. Instead, he had him put in prison until he paid back the debt. Now when his fellow servants saw what had happened, they were deeply disturbed, and went to their master and reported the whole affair. His master summoned him and said to him, 'You wicked servant! I forgave you your entire debt because you begged me to. Should you not have had pity on your fellow servant, as I had pity on you?' Then in anger his master handed him over to the torturers until he should pay back the whole debt. So will my heavenly Father do to you, unless each of you forgives your brother from your heart."

God's Word strikes the heart. What word or phrase struck your heart?

_____
_____

After Jesus teaches the disciples the Our Father, He says, "If you forgive men their transgressions, your heavenly Father will forgive you. But if you do not forgive men, neither will your heavenly Father forgive your transgressions" (Matthew 6:15). How does the master's action mirror the heavenly Father's?

_____
_____
_____

Justice enables one, beginning with God, to give to each what is due him. How did the servant act unjustly? In order for his entire debt to be forgiven, what must happen?

_____
_____
_____

MARCH 10 — TUESDAY OF THE THIRD WEEK OF LENT (CONTINUED)

Ask this question in prayer: "Jesus, you reveal to us the justice and mercy of Your heavenly Father, who forgives us seventy-seven times. Who have I failed to forgive? In what ways is my heart judgmental?" Write down what you hear Him saying to you.

_____
_____
_____

With gratitude I praise You, God, for:

_____
_____

✝ Lenten Check Point

Look back to your plan for Lent (pg. 20)
How would you describe your faithfulness to each form of penance?

FASTING: _____
_____

PRAYER: _____
_____

ALMSGIVING: _____
_____

Since the beginning of Lent, you may have experienced unplanned sacrifices. How well have you said "yes"? Write down your thoughts.

_____
_____
_____

MARCH 11 — WEDNESDAY OF THE THIRD WEEK OF LENT

MATTHEW 5:17–19

Jesus said to his disciples: "Do not think that I have come to abolish the law or the prophets. I have come not to abolish but to fulfill. Amen, I say to you, until heaven and earth pass away, not the smallest letter or the smallest part of a letter will pass from the law, until all things have taken place. Therefore, whoever breaks one of the least of these commandments and teaches others to do so will be called least in the Kingdom of heaven. But whoever obeys and teaches these commandments will be called greatest in the Kingdom of heaven."

God's Word strikes the heart. What word or phrase struck your heart?

_____
_____
_____

Jesus teaches the importance of obeying and teaching the commandments. Why is it important to both obey and teach the commandments?

_____
_____
_____

Why would the least in the kingdom be those who have taught others to break the commandments?

_____
_____
_____

Ask this question in prayer: "Jesus, to be your disciple means to obey and teach all the commandments. How have I failed to obey even the smallest part in loving God and neighbor?" Write down what you hear Him saying to you.

_____
_____
_____
_____

With gratitude I praise You, God, for:

_____
_____

MARCH 12 — THURSDAY OF THE THIRD WEEK OF LENT

LUKE 11:14-23

Jesus was driving out a demon that was mute, and when the demon had gone out, the mute man spoke and the crowds were amazed. Some of them said, "By the power of Beelzebul, the prince of demons, he drives out demons." Others, to test him, asked him for a sign from heaven. But he knew their thoughts and said to them, "Every kingdom divided against itself will be laid waste and house will fall against house. And if Satan is divided against himself, how will his kingdom stand? For you say that it is by Beelzebul that I drive out demons. If I, then, drive out demons by Beelzebul, by whom do your own people drive them out? Therefore they will be your judges. But if it is by the finger of God that I drive out demons, then the Kingdom of God has come upon you. When a strong man fully armed guards his palace, his possessions are safe. But when one stronger than he attacks and overcomes him, he takes away the armor on which he relied and distributes the spoils. Whoever is not with me is against me, and whoever does not gather with me scatters."

God's Word strikes the heart. What word or phrase struck your heart?

_____

_____

What do you think Jesus meant by saying, "Every kingdom divided against itself will be laid waste and will fall against house"?

_____

_____

Why can Jesus drive out demons "by the finger of God"?

_____

_____

Ask this question in prayer: "Jesus, most powerful, show me which virtues I need to cultivate to maintain an armor for protection against the devil." Write down what He says to you.

_____

_____

With gratitude I praise You, God, for:

_____

MARCH 13 — FRIDAY OF THE THIRD WEEK OF LENT

MARK 12:28-34

One of the scribes came to Jesus and asked him, "Which is the first of all the commandments?" Jesus replied, "The first is this: Hear, O Israel! The Lord our God is Lord alone! You shall love the Lord your God with all your heart, with all your soul, with all your mind, and with all your strength. The second is this: You shall love your neighbor as yourself. There is no other commandment greater than these." The scribe said to him, "Well said, teacher. You are right in saying, He is One and there is no other than he. And to love him with all your heart, with all your understanding, with all your strength, and to love your neighbor as yourself is worth more than all burnt offerings and sacrifices." And when Jesus saw that he answered with understanding, he said to him, "You are not far from the Kingdom of God." And no one dared to ask him any more questions.

God's Word strikes the heart. What word or phrase struck your heart?

_____

_____

Jesus acknowledges that the scribe's answer shows his understanding. Why is love of God and neighbor worth more than all burnt offering and sacrifice?

_____

_____

"You shall love your neighbor as yourself." What does this mean? How can you practically live this teaching of Jesus?

_____

_____

"Jesus, King of Kings, You said to the scribe, 'You are not far from the Kingdom of God.' What would You say to me?"

_____

_____

With gratitude I praise You, God, for:

_____

_____

MARCH 14 — SATURDAY OF THE THIRD WEEK OF LENT

LUKE 18:9-14

Jesus addressed this parable to those who were convinced of their own righteousness and despised everyone else. "Two people went up to the temple area to pray; one was a Pharisee and the other was a tax collector. The Pharisee took up his position and spoke this prayer to himself, 'O God, I thank you that I am not like the rest of humanity — greedy, dishonest, adulterous — or even like this tax collector. I fast twice a week, and I pay tithes on my whole income.' but the tax collector stood off at a distance and would not even raise his eyes to heaven but beat his breast and prayed, 'O God, be merciful to me a sinner.' I tell you, the latter went home justified, not the former; for everyone who exalts himself will be humbled, and the one who humbles himself will be exalted."

God's Word strikes the heart. What word or phrase struck your heart?

_____
_____

Describe the two people in the parable:

Pharisee: _____
_____

Tax collector: _____
_____

The Pharisee believed that his "burnt offering and sacrifices" made him righteous in God's eyes. What sins do you think prevented him from loving God and neighbor?

_____
_____
_____

Ask this question in prayer: "Jesus, merciful and just, it is easy to judge others. Show me how I need to be more merciful." Write down what He says to you.

_____
_____
_____

MARCH 14 — SATURDAY OF THE THIRD WEEK OF LENT (CONTINUED)

 With gratitude I praise You, God, for:

_____
_____

Christ Teacheth Humility, 1847, Lauder, Robert Scott / © Scottish National Gallery, Edinburgh / Bridgeman Images

A letter from Matt Hammitt...

Lent 2015

Dear Disciple of Christ,

"Truly, truly, I say to you, unless a grain of wheat falls into the earth and dies, it remains alone; but if it dies, it bears much fruit" (John 12:24).

These words of Jesus remind me of a simple truth that I try to keep close to my heart each day; that before resurrection or new life can come, there must first be death.

If we are to somehow attain the power of Christ's resurrection, as the Apostle Paul wrote, then we must also somehow share in his death. This principle doesn't only apply to death in a literal, physical sense. It's a truth that applies to many areas of our spiritual, emotional and relational lives as well.

I don't know what you're feeling or experiencing during this season of your journey, but I want to challenge you. I want you to ask God what He's calling you to put to death in your life today, so that the Holy Spirit can raise up new life in its place. It could be as obvious as a sin or a bad habit that you need to quit. Maybe it's something less obvious, like a wrong attitude or way of thinking that's standing in the way of your relationship with God and others. Maybe you simply need to put to death a wrong view of your Heavenly Father, accepting the truth that He loves you, just as you are.... something that changed my heart and life when I was twenty-seven years old.

UNITE. PRAISE. GIVE BACK.
SANCTUS REAL WILL BE PERFORMING ON 4.19.15 AT THE UNITE - DISCIPLES OF CHRIST CONCERT.
UNITECONCERT.COM | SANCTUSREAL.COM

Listen to what God is wanting to put to death in your heart and life today, and surrender to His will, for your good and His glory. If you're willing to experience Christ's death in this way, then I believe you will also begin to experience the power of His resurrection each and every day of your journey.

Matt Hammitt
(Singer, songwriter, and lead vocalist for the band Sanctus Real)

MARCH 15 — FOURTH SUNDAY OF LENT

JOHN 3:14-21

Jesus said to Nicodemus: "Just as Moses lifted up the serpent in the desert, so must the Son of Man be lifted up, so that everyone who believes in him may have eternal life."

For God so loved the world that he gave his only Son, so that everyone who believes in him might not perish but might have eternal life. For God did not send his Son into the world to condemn the world, but that the world might be saved through him. Whoever believes in him will not be condemned, but whoever does not believe has already been condemned, because he has not believed in the name of the only Son of God. And this is the verdict, that the light came into the world, but people preferred darkness to light, because their works were evil. For everyone who does wicked things hates the light and does not come toward the light, so that his works might not be exposed. But whoever lives the truth comes to the light, so that his works may be clearly seen as done in God.

God's Word strikes the heart. What word or phrase struck your heart?

___

Out of love for the world, what did God give? Why?

___

Describe the difference between those living in the light and those living in darkness.

___

"Jesus, Light of the World, enlighten my mind and heart to know and love truth. Reveal to me one area of darkness in my life." Write down what He reveals to you.

___

With gratitude I praise You, God, for:

MARCH 16 — MONDAY OF THE FOURTH WEEK OF LENT

JOHN 4:43–54

At that time Jesus left [Samaria] for Galilee. For Jesus himself testified that a prophet has no honor in his native place. When he came into Galilee, the Galileans welcomed him, since they had seen all he had done in Jerusalem at the feast; for they themselves had gone to the feast.

Then he returned to Cana in Galilee, where he had made the water wine. Now there was a royal official whose son was ill in Capernaum. When he heard that Jesus had arrived in Galilee from Judea, he went to him and asked him to come down and heal his son, who was near death. Jesus said to him, "Unless you people see signs and wonders, you will not believe." The royal official said to him, "Sir, come down before my child dies." Jesus said to him, "You may go; your son will live." The man believed what Jesus said to him and left. While the man was on his way back, his slaves met him and told him that his boy would live. He asked them when he began to recover. They told him, "The fever left him yesterday, about one in the afternoon." The father realized that just at that time Jesus had said to him, "Your son will live," and he and his whole household came to believe. Now this was the second sign Jesus did when he came to Galilee from Judea.

God's Word strikes the heart. What word or phrase struck your heart?

_____
_____

An act of faith requires one to believe and trust in God without "signs and wonders." How does the royal official practice an act of faith when Jesus says, "You may go; your son will live?"

_____
_____
_____

How did Jesus respond to his act of faith? How did the royal official respond?

_____
_____
_____

"Jesus, it is easier to believe when I see 'signs and wonders'. How does my faith need to increase so I may believe like the royal official?" Write down what you hear Him say.

_____
_____
_____

With gratitude I praise You, God, for:

_____

MARCH 17 — TUESDAY OF THE FOURTH WEEK OF LENT

JOHN 5:1–16

There was a feast of the Jews, and Jesus went up to Jerusalem. Now there is in Jerusalem at the Sheep Gate a pool called in Hebrew Bethesda, with five porticoes. In these lay a large number of ill, blind, lame, and crippled. One man was there who had been ill for thirty-eight years. When Jesus saw him lying there and knew that he had been ill for a long time, he said to him, "Do you want to be well?" The sick man answered him, "Sir, I have no one to put me into the pool when the water is stirred up; while I am on my way, someone else gets down there before me." Jesus said to him, "Rise, take up your mat, and walk." Immediately the man became well, took up his mat, and walked.

Now that day was a sabbath. So the Jews said to the man who was cured, "It is the sabbath, and it is not lawful for you to carry your mat." He answered them, "The man who made me well told me, 'Take up your mat and walk.'" They asked him, "Who is the man who told you, 'Take it up and walk'?" The man who was healed did not know who it was, for Jesus had slipped away, since there was a crowd there. After this Jesus found him in the temple area and said to him, "Look, you are well; do not sin any more, so that nothing worse may happen to you." The man went and told the Jews that Jesus was the one who had made him well. Therefore, the Jews began to persecute Jesus because he did this on a sabbath.

God's Word strikes the heart. What word or phrase struck your heart?

_____
_____

Why do you think Jesus knew how long the man had been at the pool? [Hint: Ann and Joachim, His grandparents, lived near there.]

_____
_____
_____

Jesus asked the man, "Do you want to be well?" What did Jesus tell him to do?

_____
_____
_____

After his healing, Jesus sees him again. What does He say to him?

_____
_____
_____

The man is healed once he picks up his mat. Ask Jesus these questions in prayer: "How can I be healed by willingly accepting my illness or suffering? Is there something in my life which is preventing me from freely walking as a disciple of Christ?"

_____
_____
_____
_____

☩ With gratitude I praise You, God, for:

_____
_____

✝ Lenten Check Point

Life is filled with many distractions which prevents us from listening to Jesus. He may be asking you, "Do you want to be well?" For the next week try to unplug for a period of time from a device.

MARCH 18 — WEDNESDAY OF THE FOURTH WEEK OF LENT

JOHN 5:17-30

Jesus answered the Jews: "My Father is at work until now, so I am at work." For this reason they tried all the more to kill him, because he not only broke the sabbath but he also called God his own father, making himself equal to God.

Jesus answered and said to them, "Amen, amen, I say to you, the Son cannot do anything on his own, but only what he sees the Father doing; for what he does, the Son will do also. For the Father loves the Son and shows him everything that he himself does, and he will show him greater works than these, so that you may be amazed. For just as the Father raises the dead and gives life, so also does the Son give life to whomever he wishes. Nor does the Father judge anyone, but he has given all judgment to the Son, so that all may honor the Son just as they honor the Father. Whoever does not honor the Son does not honor the Father who sent him. Amen, amen, I say to you, whoever hears my word and believes in the one who sent me has eternal life and will not come to condemnation, but has passed from death to life. Amen, amen, I say to you, the hour is coming and is now here when the dead will hear the voice of the Son of God, and those who hear will live. For just as the Father has life in himself, so also he gave to the Son the possession of life in himself. And he gave him power to exercise judgment, because he is the Son of Man. Do not be amazed at this, because the hour is coming in which all who are in the tombs will hear his voice and will come out, those who have done good deeds to the resurrection of life, but those who have done wicked deeds to the resurrection of condemnation.

"I cannot do anything on my own; I judge as I hear, and my judgment is just, because I do not seek my own will but the will of the one who sent me."

God's Word strikes the heart. What word or phrase struck your heart?

_____
_____
_____

Jesus' words deeply disturbed the Jews, and they wanted to kill Him. Despite their anger, Jesus answered them. What does His teaching reveal to us about God the Father?

_____
_____
_____

With gratitude I praise You, God, for:

_____
_____

Jesus, Your word and deeds reveal to me the heart of God the Father. Help me to know and believe in His love for me.

MARCH 19 — THURSDAY OF THE FOURTH WEEK OF LENT

MATTHEW 1:16, 18–21, 24A
(LUKE 2:41–51A)

Jacob was the father of Joseph, the husband of Mary. Of her was born Jesus who is called the Christ.

Now this is how the birth of Jesus Christ came about. When his mother Mary was betrothed to Joseph, but before they lived together, she was found with child through the Holy Spirit. Joseph her husband, since he was a righteous man, yet unwilling to expose her to shame, decided to divorce her quietly. Such was his intention when, behold, the angel of the Lord appeared to him in a dream and said, "Joseph, son of David, do not be afraid to take Mary your wife into your home. For it is through the Holy Spirit that this child has been conceived in her. She will bear a son and you are to name him Jesus, because he will save his people from their sins." When Joseph awoke, he did as the angel of the Lord had commanded him and took his wife into his home.

God's Word strikes the heart. What word or phrase struck your heart?

_____
_____

The angel of the Lord appeared to Joseph in a dream. Why do you think Joseph was afraid to take Mary into his home?

_____
_____

Describe the virtues Joseph possessed which enabled him to respond to the words of the angel.

_____
_____

"Jesus, Your foster father, Joseph, was a model of virtue and responded to the will of Your Father. In what ways can I imitate him so as to faithfully love and serve You as he did?" Write down what He says to you.

_____
_____
_____

MARCH 19 — THURSDAY OF THE FOURTH WEEK OF LENT (CONTINUED)

✝ With gratitude I praise You, God, for:

_____

_____

The Dream of St. Joseph, Rembrandt Harmensz. van Rijn / Museum of Fine Arts, Budapest, Hungary / Interfoto / Bridgeman Images

MARCH 20 — FRIDAY OF THE FOURTH WEEK OF LENT

JOHN 7:1-2, 10, 25-30

Jesus moved about within Galilee; he did not wish to travel in Judea, because the Jews were trying to kill him. But the Jewish feast of Tabernacles was near.

But when his brothers had gone up to the feast, he himself also went up, not openly but as it were in secret.

Some of the inhabitants of Jerusalem said, "Is he not the one they are trying to kill? And look, he is speaking openly and they say nothing to him. Could the authorities have realized that he is the Christ? But we know where he is from. When the Christ comes, no one will know where he is from." So Jesus cried out in the temple area as he was teaching and said, "You know me and also know where I am from. Yet I did not come on my own, but the one who sent me, whom you do not know, is true. I know him, because I am from him, and he sent me." So they tried to arrest him, but no one laid a hand upon him, because his hour had not yet come.

God's Word strikes the heart. What word or phrase struck your heart?

_____
_____
_____

Jesus continues to preach to those in Galilee. Yet when He traveled in Judea, He was rejected by the Jews. Why do you think John described in detail how Jesus cried out in the temple area?

_____
_____
_____

Ask this question in prayer: "Jesus, despite the rejection of the Jews, You continued to teach and proclaim the truth. It can be hard and discouraging to speak and have other people reject truth. How can I cultivate the virtues of fortitude and perseverance in my daily life?" Write down what He says to you.

_____
_____
_____

With gratitude I praise You, God, for:

_____
_____

MARCH 21 — SATURDAY OF THE FOURTH WEEK OF LENT

JOHN 7:40–53

Some in the crowd who heard these words of Jesus said, "This is truly the Prophet." Others said, "This is the Christ." But others said, "The Christ will not come from Galilee, will he? Does not Scripture say that the Christ will be of David's family and come from Bethlehem, the village where David lived?" So a division occurred in the crowd because of him. Some of them even wanted to arrest him, but no one laid hands on him.

So the guards went to the chief priests and Pharisees, who asked them, "Why did you not bring him?" The guards answered, "Never before has anyone spoken like this man." So the Pharisees answered them, "Have you also been deceived? Have any of the authorities or the Pharisees believed in him? But this crowd, which does not know the law, is accursed." Nicodemus, one of their members who had come to him earlier, said to them, "Does our law condemn a man before it first hears him and finds out what he is doing?" They answered and said to him, "You are not from Galilee also, are you? Look and see that no prophet arises from Galilee."

Then each went to his own house.

God's Word strikes the heart. What word or phrase struck your heart?

___

Describe how the different people in the crowd respond to Jesus.

___

John wrote about Nicodemus' visit to Jesus at night (John 3:1–21). Why do think his reaction is different?

___

"Jesus, even today people react differently to you. Some accept you as the Christ, and many do not. Nicodemus had a docile heart and a courageous spirit. How can I live more faithfully as Your disciple?" Write down what you hear Him say to you.

___

With gratitude I praise You, God, for:

___

MARCH 22 — FIFTH SUNDAY OF LENT

JOHN 12:20-33

Some Greeks who had come to worship at the Passover Feast came to Philip, who was from Bethsaida in Galilee, and asked him, "Sir, we would like to see Jesus." Philip went and told Andrew; then Andrew and Philip went and told Jesus. Jesus answered them, "The hour has come for the Son of Man to be glorified. Amen, amen, I say to you, unless a grain of wheat falls to the ground and dies, it remains just a grain of wheat; but if it dies, it produces much fruit. Whoever loves his life loses it, and whoever hates his life in this world will preserve it for eternal life. Whoever serves me must follow me, and where I am, there also will my servant be. The Father will honor whoever serves me.

"I am troubled now. Yet what should I say? 'Father, save me from this hour'? But it was for this purpose that I came to this hour. Father, glorify your name." Then a voice came from heaven, "I have glorified it and will glorify it again." The crowd there heard it and said it was thunder; but others said, "An angel has spoken to him." Jesus answered and said, "This voice did not come for my sake but for yours. Now is the time of judgment on this world; now the ruler of this world will be driven out. And when I am lifted up from the earth, I will draw everyone to myself." He said this indicating the kind of death he would die.

God's Word strikes the heart. What word or phrase struck your heart?

_____
_____

The Greeks were seeking to see Jesus, and yet He answers them by describing how one must be willing to follow Him. What does He teach them about the grain of wheat?

_____
_____

Look carefully at the facial expressions in the picture. How would you have reacted if you heard Him speak about His death and glorification as well as hear a voice from heaven?

_____
_____

✝ With gratitude I praise You, God, for:

_____
_____

MARCH 22 — FIFTH SUNDAY OF LENT (CONTINUED)

The Voice from Heaven, illustration for The Life of Christ, Tissot, James Jacques Joseph / Brooklyn Museum of Art, New York, USA / Bridgeman Images

Jesus, sometimes it is hard to understand Your teachings, and sometimes it is very difficult to die to myself and follow You. Teach me what I need to do to serve and follow You.

MARCH 23 — MONDAY OF THE FIFTH WEEK OF LENT

JOHN 8:1-11

Jesus went to the Mount of Olives. But early in the morning he arrived again in the temple area, and all the people started coming to him, and he sat down and taught them. Then the scribes and the Pharisees brought a woman who had been caught in adultery and made her stand in the middle. They said to him, "Teacher, this woman was caught in the very act of committing adultery. Now in the law, Moses commanded us to stone such women. So what do you say?" They said this to test him, so that they could have some charge to bring against him. Jesus bent down and began to write on the ground with his finger. But when they continued asking him, he straightened up and said to them, "Let the one among you who is without sin be the first to throw a stone at her." Again he bent down and wrote on the ground. And in response, they went away one by one, beginning with the elders. So he was left alone with the woman before him. Then Jesus straightened up and said to her, "Woman, where are they? Has no one condemned you?" She replied, "No one, sir." Then Jesus said, "Neither do I condemn you. Go, and from now on do not sin any more."

God's Word strikes the heart. What word or phrase struck your heart?

_____
_____

What do you think the scribes and Pharisees expected Jesus to do?

_____
_____

With His finger, Jesus writes on the ground, and everyone drops their stones and walks away. What do you think Jesus wrote?

_____
_____

"Jesus, You said that by the 'finger of God' You cast out demons. Touch my heart with Your finger so that You may cast out any demons which prevent me from loving You and others. What stones of sin and judgment do I need to let go of?" Write down what He says to you.

_____
_____

With gratitude I praise You, God, for:

_____
_____

MARCH 24 — TUESDAY OF THE FIFTH WEEK OF LENT

JOHN 8:21-30

Jesus said to the Pharisees: "I am going away and you will look for me, but you will die in your sin. Where I am going you cannot come." So the Jews said, "He is not going to kill himself, is he, because he said, 'Where I am going you cannot come'?" He said to them, "You belong to what is below, I belong to what is above. You belong to this world, but I do not belong to this world. That is why I told you that you will die in your sins. For if you do not believe that I AM, you will die in your sins." So they said to him, "Who are you?" Jesus said to them, "What I told you from the beginning. I have much to say about you in condemnation. But the one who sent me is true, and what I heard from him I tell the world." They did not realize that he was speaking to them of the Father. So Jesus said to them, "When you lift up the Son of Man, then you will realize that I AM, and that I do nothing on my own, but I say only what the Father taught me. The one who sent me is with me. He has not left me alone, because I always do what is pleasing to him." Because he spoke this way, many came to believe in him.

God's Word strikes the heart. What word or phrase struck your heart?

_____

_____

How does Jesus respond to the Jews' question, "Who are you?"

_____

_____

Why is it essential for them and for us to believe that Jesus is "I AM?"

_____

_____

"Jesus, You instruct us in the ways that You are 'I AM'. Reveal to me one way in which I need to ponder within my heart, 'I am the Vine,' 'I am the Good Shepherd,' 'I am the Bread of Life,' 'I am the Light of the World,' 'I am the Resurrection,' 'I am the Way, the Truth, and the Life'. Write down what you hear Him say to you.

_____

_____

_____

With gratitude I praise You, God, for:

_____

MARCH 25 — WEDNESDAY OF THE FIFTH WEEK OF LENT

LUKE 1:26-38

The angel Gabriel was sent from God to a town of Galilee called Nazareth, to a virgin betrothed to a man named Joseph, of the house of David, and the virgin's name was Mary. And coming to her, he said, "Hail, full of grace! The Lord is with you." But she was greatly troubled at what was said and pondered what sort of greeting this might be. Then the angel said to her, "Do not be afraid, Mary, for you have found favor with God. Behold, you will conceive in your womb and bear a son, and you shall name him Jesus. He will be great and will be called Son of the Most High, and the Lord God will give him the throne of David his father, and he will rule over the house of Jacob forever, and of his Kingdom there will be no end." But Mary said to the angel, "How can this be, since I have no relations with a man?" And the angel said to her in reply, "The Holy Spirit will come upon you, and the power of the Most High will overshadow you. Therefore the child to be born will be called holy, the Son of God. And behold, Elizabeth, your relative, has also conceived a son in her old age, and this is the sixth month for her who was called barren; for nothing will be impossible for God." Mary said, "Behold, I am the handmaid of the Lord. May it be done to me according to your word." Then the angel departed from her.

God's Word strikes the heart. What word or phrase struck your heart?

_____
_____

St. Luke, a doctor, provides details about Mary and Elizabeth that emphasize the words of the angel Gabriel, "For nothing will be impossible for God." What are these details about Mary and Elizabeth? How did God intervene?

_____
_____
_____

Ask Jesus this question in prayer, "Jesus, Your mother prayerfully pondered Gabriel's message. How can I be more patient and ponder God's will for my life?" Write down what you hear Him say to you.

_____
_____

With gratitude I praise You, God, for:

_____
_____

MARCH 25 — WEDNESDAY OF THE FIFTH WEEK OF LENT

The Annunciation, 17th century, Murillo, Bartolome Esteban / Prado, Madrid, Spain / Bridgeman Images

MARCH 26 — THURSDAY OF THE FIFTH WEEK OF LENT

JOHN 8:51-59

Jesus said to the Jews: "Amen, amen, I say to you, whoever keeps my word will never see death." So the Jews said to him, "Now we are sure that you are possessed. Abraham died, as did the prophets, yet you say, 'Whoever keeps my word will never taste death.' Are you greater than our father Abraham, who died? Or the prophets, who died? Who do you make yourself out to be?" Jesus answered, "If I glorify myself, my glory is worth nothing; but it is my Father who glorifies me, of whom you say, 'He is our God.' You do not know him, but I know him. And if I should say that I do not know him, I would be like you a liar. But I do know him and I keep his word. Abraham your father rejoiced to see my day; he saw it and was glad." So the Jews said to him, "You are not yet fifty years old and you have seen Abraham?" Jesus said to them, "Amen, amen, I say to you, before Abraham came to be, I AM." So they picked up stones to throw at him; but Jesus hid and went out of the temple area.

God's Word strikes the heart. What word or phrase struck your heart?

_____
_____

Jesus reveals to us the means to obtaining eternal life: "to never see death." What does it mean to "keep my word"?

_____
_____

Jesus reveals further His relationship with His Father by stating that He knows Him and keeps His word. How do the Jews respond to Him?

_____
_____

Ask this question in prayer: "Jesus, Son of the Living Father, You have taught us that our happiness lies in honoring and keeping the word (see Luke 11:27–28). How can I be a better listener to Your Word so I may keep it in my heart?" Write down what He says to you.

_____
_____

With gratitude I praise You, God, for:

_____
_____

MARCH 27 — FRIDAY OF THE FIFTH WEEK OF LENT

JOHN 10:31–42

The Jews picked up rocks to stone Jesus. Jesus answered them, "I have shown you many good works from my Father. For which of these are you trying to stone me?" The Jews answered him, "We are not stoning you for a good work but for blasphemy. You, a man, are making yourself God." Jesus answered them, "Is it not written in your law, 'I said, "You are gods"'? If it calls them gods to whom the word of God came, and Scripture cannot be set aside, can you say that the one whom the Father has consecrated and sent into the world blasphemes because I said, 'I am the Son of God'? If I do not perform my Father's works, do not believe me; but if I perform them, even if you do not believe me, believe the works, so that you may realize and understand that the Father is in me and I am in the Father." Then they tried again to arrest him; but he escaped from their power.

He went back across the Jordan to the place where John first baptized, and there he remained. Many came to him and said, "John performed no sign, but everything John said about this man was true." And many there began to believe in him.

God's Word strikes the heart. What word or phrase struck your heart?

_____
_____

Jesus continues to witness by His words and deeds, but the Jews do not have "ears that hear". Why do they threaten to stone Him or have Him arrested?

_____
_____
_____

When Jesus departed Jerusalem and crossed the Jordan river, how was He received?

_____
_____
_____

Describe the difference between the Jews and those who came to see Jesus.

_____
_____
_____

MARCH 27 — FRIDAY OF THE FIFTH WEEK OF LENT

Ask this question in prayer: "Jesus, those who were baptized by John had recognized their sins and repented. How am I in need of repentance so I may seek You more fully?" Write down what He says to you.

_____

_____

 With gratitude I praise You, God, for:

_____

_____

_____

The Jews took up Stones to Cast at Him, illustration for *The Life of Christ*, Tissot, James Jacques Joseph / Brooklyn Museum of Art, New York, USA / Bridgeman Images

MARCH 28 — SATURDAY OF THE FIFTH WEEK OF LENT

JOHN 11:45–56

Many of the Jews who had come to Mary and seen what Jesus had done began to believe in him. But some of them went to the Pharisees and told them what Jesus had done. So the chief priests and the Pharisees convened the Sanhedrin and said, "What are we going to do? This man is performing many signs. If we leave him alone, all will believe in him, and the Romans will come and take away both our land and our nation." But one of them, Caiaphas, who was high priest that year, said to them, "You know nothing, nor do you consider that it is better for you that one man should die instead of the people, so that the whole nation may not perish." He did not say this on his own, but since he was high priest for that year, he prophesied that Jesus was going to die for the nation, and not only for the nation, but also to gather into one the dispersed children of God. So from that day on they planned to kill him.

So Jesus no longer walked about in public among the Jews, but he left for the region near the desert, to a town called Ephraim, and there he remained with his disciples.

Now the Passover of the Jews was near, and many went up from the country to Jerusalem before Passover to purify themselves. They looked for Jesus and said to one another as they were in the temple area, "What do you think? That he will not come to the feast?"

God's Word strikes the heart. What word or phrase struck your heart?

_____
_____
_____

The Jews went to Mary because they had witnessed Jesus raising Lazarus from the dead. Jesus' words and deeds continued to divide the Jews, so they went to the Sanhedrin. Describe their fears and confusion.

_____
_____
_____
_____

If you were a member of the Sanhedrin, how would you have responded to the question, "What are we going to do?"

_____
_____
_____
_____

MARCH 28 — SATURDAY OF THE FIFTH WEEK OF LENT (CONTINUED)

Jesus experienced rejection and knows how it feels to be hated by people. Think about a time you have felt rejected or hurt by other people. Write a short prayer to Jesus about your feelings.

_____
_____
_____

With gratitude I praise You, God, for:

_____
_____
_____

✝ Lenten Check Point

The days of Lent prepare us to journey with Christ through His Passion, Death and Resurrection. If you have not faithfully lived your plan for Lent, renew your intentions and strive to be with Jesus this week. Write a prayer expressing your intentions.

_____
_____
_____
_____

A letter from Jon...

Lent 2015

Dear Disciple of Christ,

"Let love find you, as it certainly will, for we at our supremest are but its trembling emblems."

Emily Dickinson wrote that in a letter to a friend who was off at war. He was frightened by the brutality and horror of his experience, and his friend wrote him of love. I can only imagine what the young soldier would have thought after reading this for the first time. "What does love have to do with war?"

Love is a bit of an elastic word. It bends with us, conforming itself to whatever use we might make of it. "I love sushi. I love summertime. I love that song. I love her. I love him. I love you. I love God." But that doesn't mean it has no meaning. It means love is multi-dimensional. It means love is big enough to encompass the whole of our human experience, even the most mundane.

God says life can be summed up in two commands: love God with everything you have, and love your neighbor as yourself. Those two things take a lifetime to learn. But God didn't leave us without an example.

"But God demonstrates his own love for us in this: While we were still sinners, Christ died for us" (Romans 5:8).

God suffered greatly...for us. The cross is at the center of His love, proving that we are not alone, but that we are loved to the ultimate degree. The resurrection of Jesus proves that this manner of love is absolutely worth the sacrifice.

UNITE. PRAISE. GIVE BACK.
JON GUERRA WILL BE PERFORMING ON 4.19.15 AT THE UNITE - DISCIPLES OF CHRIST CONCERT.
UNITECONCERT.COM | JONGUERRAMUSIC.COM

This is the manner of love that God invites us into: a self-sacrificing, unconditional, and fundamentally gracious love. It hurts sometimes, as it did for Christ on the cross. But we have resurrection hope assuring us that no sacrificial love done in the name of Christ will be lost or forgotten. For Christians who love, resurrection is just around the corner. For love has indeed found us and we, at our best, are but its trembling emblems.

Jon Guerra

MARCH 29 — PALM SUNDAY OF THE LORD'S PASSION

MARK 15:1–39 (OR MARK 14:1–15:47)

As soon as morning came, the chief priests with the elders and the scribes, that is, the whole Sanhedrin held a council. They bound Jesus, led him away, and handed him over to Pilate. Pilate questioned him, "Are you the king of the Jews?" He said to him in reply, "You say so." The chief priests accused him of many things. Again Pilate questioned him, "Have you no answer? See how many things they accuse you of." Jesus gave him no further answer, so that Pilate was amazed.

Now on the occasion of the feast he used to release to them one prisoner whom they requested. A man called Barabbas was then in prison along with the rebels who had committed murder in a rebellion. The crowd came forward and began to ask him to do for them as he was accustomed. Pilate answered, "Do you want me to release to you the king of the Jews?" For he knew that it was out of envy that the chief priests had handed him over. But the chief priests stirred up the crowd to have him release Barabbas for them instead. Pilate again said to them in reply, "Then what do you want me to do with the man you call the king of the Jews?" They shouted again, "Crucify him." Pilate said to them, "Why? What evil has he done?" They only shouted the louder, "Crucify him." So Pilate, wishing to satisfy the crowd, released Barabbas to them and, after he had Jesus scourged, handed him over to be crucified.

The soldiers led him away inside the palace, that is, the praetorium, and assembled the whole cohort. They clothed him in purple and, weaving a crown of thorns, placed it on him. They began to salute him with, "Hail, King of the Jews!" and kept striking his head with a reed and spitting upon him. They knelt before him in homage. And when they had mocked him, they stripped him of the purple cloak, dressed him in his own clothes, and led him out to crucify him.

They pressed into service a passer-by, Simon, a Cyrenian, who was coming in from the country, the father of Alexander and Rufus, to carry his cross.

They brought him to the place of Golgotha — which is translated Place of the Skull ---. They gave him wine drugged with myrrh, but he did not take it. Then they crucified him and divided his garments by casting lots for them to see what each should take. It was nine o'clock in the morning when they crucified him. The inscription of the charge against him read, "The King of the Jews." With him they crucified two revolutionaries, one on his right and one on his left. Those passing by reviled him, shaking their heads and saying, "Aha! You who would destroy the temple and rebuild it in three days, save yourself by coming down from the cross." Likewise the chief priests, with the scribes, mocked him among themselves and said, "He saved others; he cannot save himself. Let the Christ, the King of Israel, come down now from the cross that we may see and believe." Those who were crucified with him also kept abusing him.

At noon darkness came over the whole land until three in the afternoon. And at three o'clock Jesus cried out in a loud voice, "Eloi, Eloi, lema sabachthani?" which is translated, "My God, my God, why have you forsaken me?" Some of the bystanders who heard it said, "Look, he is calling Elijah." One of them ran, soaked a sponge with wine, put it on a reed and gave it to him to drink saying, "Wait, let us see if Elijah comes to take him down." Jesus gave a loud cry and breathed his last.

[Here all kneel and pause for a short time.]

The veil of the sanctuary was torn in two from top to bottom. When the centurion who stood facing him saw how he breathed his last he said, "Truly this man was the Son of God!"

MARCH 29 — PSALM SUNDAY OF THE LORD'S PASSION (CONTINUED)

🙏 *Spend time meditating upon the Lord's Passion.*

God's Word strikes the heart. What word or phrase struck your heart?

_____
_____

The word compassion means to "suffer with." Place yourself in one of the scenes and write about how you would have felt if you witnessed the suffering of Jesus.

_____
_____
_____
_____
_____
_____

In prayer say to Jesus: "Jesus, You have experienced suffering to the core of Your being. Help me to believe that You have compassion for me when I suffer." Write down ways you will know of His promise.

_____
_____
_____

🙌 With gratitude I praise You, God, for:

_____
_____
_____

MARCH 30 — MONDAY OF HOLY WEEK

JOHN 12:1-11

Six days before Passover Jesus came to Bethany, where Lazarus was, whom Jesus had raised from the dead. They gave a dinner for him there, and Martha served, while Lazarus was one of those reclining at table with him. Mary took a liter of costly perfumed oil made from genuine aromatic nard and anointed the feet of Jesus and dried them with her hair; the house was filled with the fragrance of the oil. Then Judas the Iscariot, one of his disciples, and the one who would betray him, said, "Why was this oil not sold for three hundred days' wages and given to the poor?" He said this not because he cared about the poor but because he was a thief and held the money bag and used to steal the contributions. So Jesus said, "Leave her alone. Let her keep this for the day of my burial. You always have the poor with you, but you do not always have me."

The large crowd of the Jews found out that he was there and came, not only because of him, but also to see Lazarus, whom he had raised from the dead. And the chief priests plotted to kill Lazarus too, because many of the Jews were turning away and believing in Jesus because of him.

God's Word strikes the heart. What word or phrase struck your heart?

_____

Describe the action of Mary.

_____

Describe the reaction of Judas.

_____

With gratitude I praise You, God, for:

_____

MARCH 31 — TUESDAY OF HOLY WEEK

JOHN 13:21-33, 36-38

Reclining at table with his disciples, Jesus was deeply troubled and testified, "Amen, amen, I say to you, one of you will betray me." The disciples looked at one another, at a loss as to whom he meant. One of his disciples, the one whom Jesus loved, was reclining at Jesus' side. So Simon Peter nodded to him to find out whom he meant. He leaned back against Jesus' chest and said to him, "Master, who is it?" Jesus answered, "It is the one to whom I hand the morsel after I have dipped it." So he dipped the morsel and took it and handed it to Judas, son of Simon the Iscariot. After Judas took the morsel, Satan entered him. So Jesus said to him, "What you are going to do, do quickly." Now none of those reclining at table realized why he said this to him. Some thought that since Judas kept the money bag, Jesus had told him, "Buy what we need for the feast," or to give something to the poor. So Judas took the morsel and left at once. And it was night.

When he had left, Jesus said, "Now is the Son of Man glorified, and God is glorified in him. If God is glorified in him, God will also glorify him in himself, and he will glorify him at once. My children, I will be with you only a little while longer. You will look for me, and as I told the Jews, 'Where I go you cannot come,' so now I say it to you."

Simon Peter said to him, "Master, where are you going?" Jesus answered him, "Where I am going, you cannot follow me now, though you will follow later." Peter said to him, "Master, why can I not follow you now? I will lay down my life for you." Jesus answered, "Will you lay down your life for me? Amen, amen, I say to you, the cock will not crow before you deny me three times."

God's Word strikes the heart. What word or phrase struck your heart?

_____
_____

Even though Judas was a disciple of Christ, Satan was able to enter his heart. Why?

_____
_____
_____

Look back to page 57. Have you tried to cultivate the virtues to secure the armor of protection for your heart?

_____
_____
_____

MARCH 31 — TUESDAY OF HOLY WEEK (CONTINUED)

In prayer, say to Jesus: "Jesus, You loved Judas and Peter. Judas betrayed You and Peter would deny knowing You. Sadly, Judas did not believe in Your mercy and forgiveness, but Peter did." Write a prayer asking Jesus to teach you how to know and trust in His mercy.

_____
_____
_____
_____

With gratitude I praise You, God, for:

_____
_____
_____

The Last Supper. Judas Dipping His Hand in the Dish, illustration for *The Life of Christ*, Tissot, James Jacques Joseph / Brooklyn Museum of Art, New York, USA / Bridgeman Images

APRIL 1 — WEDNESDAY OF HOLY WEEK

MATTHEW 26:14-25

One of the Twelve, who was called Judas Iscariot, went to the chief priests and said, "What are you willing to give me if I hand him over to you?" They paid him thirty pieces of silver, and from that time on he looked for an opportunity to hand him over.

On the first day of the Feast of Unleavened Bread, the disciples approached Jesus and said, "Where do you want us to prepare for you to eat the Passover?" He said, "Go into the city to a certain man and tell him, 'The teacher says, "My appointed time draws near; in your house I shall celebrate the Passover with my disciples."'" The disciples then did as Jesus had ordered, and prepared the Passover.

When it was evening, he reclined at table with the Twelve. And while they were eating, he said, "Amen, I say to you, one of you will betray me." Deeply distressed at this, they began to say to him one after another, "Surely it is not I, Lord?" He said in reply, "He who has dipped his hand into the dish with me is the one who will betray me. The Son of Man indeed goes, as it is written of him, but woe to that man by whom the Son of Man is betrayed. It would be better for that man if he had never been born." Then Judas, his betrayer, said in reply, "Surely it is not I, Rabbi?" He answered, "You have said so."

God's Word strikes the heart. What word or phrase struck your heart?

_____
_____

Recall how Judas had complained about the oil worth three hundred days' wages being poured out in the anointing. Now he betrays Christ for thirty pieces of silver. What does this show about Judas?

_____
_____
_____

When Jesus describes the person who will betray him, He says, "It would be better for that man if he had never been born." What do you think this means?

_____
_____
_____

APRIL 1 — WEDNESDAY OF HOLY WEEK (CONTINUED)

"Jesus, Judas states, 'Surely it is not I, Rabbi?' which indicates a denial of his betrayal of the heart. Show me how my sins have betrayed You and give me the grace of repentance." Write down what He reveals to you.

_____
_____
_____
_____

With gratitude I praise You, God, for:

_____
_____
_____

The Payment of Judas, c.1305 (fresco), Giotto di Bondone / Scrovegni (Arena) Chapel, Padua, Italy / Bridgeman Images

APRIL 2 — HOLY THURSDAY EVENING MASS OF THE LORD'S SUPPER

JOHN 13:1–15

Before the feast of Passover, Jesus knew that his hour had come to pass from this world to the Father. He loved his own in the world and he loved them to the end. The devil had already induced Judas, son of Simon the Iscariot, to hand him over. So, during supper, fully aware that the Father had put everything into his power and that he had come from God and was returning to God, he rose from supper and took off his outer garments. He took a towel and tied it around his waist. Then he poured water into a basin and began to wash the disciples' feet and dry them with the towel around his waist. He came to Simon Peter, who said to him, "Master, are you going to wash my feet?" Jesus answered and said to him, "What I am doing, you do not understand now, but you will understand later." Peter said to him, "You will never wash my feet." Jesus answered him, "Unless I wash you, you will have no inheritance with me." Simon Peter said to him, "Master, then not only my feet, but my hands and head as well." Jesus said to him, "Whoever has bathed has no need except to have his feet washed, for he is clean all over; so you are clean, but not all." For he knew who would betray him; for this reason, he said, "Not all of you are clean."

So when he had washed their feet and put his garments back on and reclined at table again, he said to them, "Do you realize what I have done for you? You call me 'teacher' and 'master,' and rightly so, for indeed I am. If I, therefore, the master and teacher, have washed your feet, you ought to wash one another's feet. I have given you a model to follow, so that as I have done for you, you should also do."

God's Word strikes the heart. What word or phrase struck your heart?

___

Even though the devil has entered Judas' heart to betray Him, Jesus continues to teach the disciples how to live. What does the washing of the disciples' feet show about Jesus? What virtues are exemplified?

___

How are you called to "wash the feet" of other people?

___

APRIL 2 — HOLY THURSDAY (CONTINUED)

Ask this question in prayer: "Jesus, meek and humble of heart, You give yourself to us in the Eucharist. How can I draw closer to You and give of myself to others?" Write down what He says to you.

_____
_____
_____
_____

 With gratitude I praise You, God, for:

_____
_____

Jesus Washing Peter's Feet, Brown, Ford Mado / Manchester Art Gallery, UK / Bridgeman Images

APRIL 3 — FRIDAY OF THE PASSION OF THE LORD (GOOD FRIDAY)

JOHN 18:1–19:42

Jesus went out with his disciples across the Kidron valley to where there was a garden, into which he and his disciples entered. Judas his betrayer also knew the place, because Jesus had often met there with his disciples. So Judas got a band of soldiers and guards from the chief priests and the Pharisees and went there with lanterns, torches, and weapons. Jesus, knowing everything that was going to happen to him, went out and said to them, "Whom are you looking for?" They answered him, "Jesus the Nazorean." He said to them, "I AM." Judas his betrayer was also with them. When he said to them, "I AM," they turned away and fell to the ground. So he again asked them, "Whom are you looking for?" They said, "Jesus the Nazorean." Jesus answered, "I told you that I AM. So if you are looking for me, let these men go." This was to fulfill what he had said, "I have not lost any of those you gave me." Then Simon Peter, who had a sword, drew it, struck the high priest's slave, and cut off his right ear. The slave's name was Malchus. Jesus said to Peter, "Put your sword into its scabbard. Shall I not drink the cup that the Father gave me?"

So the band of soldiers, the tribune, and the Jewish guards seized Jesus, bound him, and brought him to Annas first. He was the father-in-law of Caiaphas, who was high priest that year. It was Caiaphas who had counseled the Jews that it was better that one man should die rather than the people.

Simon Peter and another disciple followed Jesus. Now the other disciple was known to the high priest, and he entered the courtyard of the high priest with Jesus. But Peter stood at the gate outside. So the other disciple, the acquaintance of the high priest, went out and spoke to the gatekeeper and brought Peter in. Then the maid who was the gatekeeper said to Peter, "You are not one of this man's disciples, are you?" He said, "I am not." Now the slaves and the guards were standing around a charcoal fire that they had made, because it was cold, and were warming themselves. Peter was also standing there keeping warm.

The high priest questioned Jesus about his disciples and about his doctrine. Jesus answered him, "I have spoken publicly to the world. I have always taught in a synagogue or in the temple area where all the Jews gather, and in secret I have said nothing. Why ask me? Ask those who heard me what I said to them. They know what I said." When he had said this, one of the temple guards standing there struck Jesus and said, "Is this the way you answer the high priest?" Jesus answered him, "If I have spoken wrongly, testify to the wrong; but if I have spoken rightly, why do you strike me?" Then Annas sent him bound to Caiaphas the high priest.

Now Simon Peter was standing there keeping warm. And they said to him, "You are not one of his disciples, are you?" He denied it and said, "I am not." One of the slaves of the high priest, a relative of the one whose ear Peter had cut off, said, "Didn't I see you in the garden with him?" Again Peter denied it. And immediately the cock crowed.

Then they brought Jesus from Caiaphas to the praetorium. It was morning. And they themselves did not enter the praetorium, in order not to be defiled so that they could eat the Passover. So Pilate came out to them and said, "What charge do you bring against this man?" They answered and said to him, "If he were not a criminal, we would not have handed him over to you." At this, Pilate said to them, "Take him yourselves, and judge him according to your law." Then Jews answered him, "We do not have the right to execute anyone," in order that the word of Jesus might be fulfilled that he said indicating the kind of death he would die. So Pilate went back into the praetorium and summoned

APRIL 3 — FRIDAY OF THE PASSION OF THE LORD (GOOD FRIDAY) (CONTINUED)

Jesus and said to him, "Are you the King of the Jews?" Jesus answered, "Do you say this on your own or have others told you about me?" Pilate answered, "I am not a Jew, am I? Your own nation and the chief priests handed you over to me. What have you done?" Jesus answered, "My kingdom does not belong to this world. If my kingdom did belong to this world, my attendants would be fighting to keep me from being handed over to the Jews. But as it is, my kingdom is not here." So Pilate said to him, "Then you are a king?" Jesus answered, "You say I am a king. For this I was born and for this I came into the world, to testify to the truth. Everyone who belongs to the truth listens to my voice." Pilate said to him, "What is truth?"

When he had said this, he again went out to the Jews and said to them, "I find no guilt in him. But you have a custom that I release one prisoner to you at Passover. Do you want me to release to you the King of the Jews?" They cried out again, "Not this one but Barabbas!" Now Barabbas was a revolutionary.

Then Pilate took Jesus and had him scourged. And the soldiers wove a crown out of thorns and placed it on his head, and clothed him in a purple cloak, and they came to him and said, "Hail, King of the Jews!" And they struck him repeatedly. Once more Pilate went out and said to them, "Look, I am bringing him out to you, so that you may know that I find no guilt in him." So Jesus came out, wearing the crown of thorns and the purple cloak. And he said to them, "Behold, the man!" When the chief priests and the guards saw him they cried out, "Crucify him, crucify him!" Pilate said to them, "Take him yourselves and crucify him. I find no guilt in him." The Jews answered, "We have a law, and according to that law he ought to die, because he made himself the Son of God." Now when Pilate heard this statement, he became even more afraid, and went back into the praetorium and said to Jesus, "Where are you from?" Jesus did not answer him. So Pilate said to him, "Do you not speak to me? Do you not know that I have power to release you and I have power to crucify you?" Jesus answered him, "You would have no power over me if it had not been given to you from above. For this reason the one who handed me over to you has the greater sin." Consequently, Pilate tried to release him; but the Jews cried out, "If you release him, you are not a friend of Caesar. Everyone who makes himself a king opposes Caesar."

When Pilate heard these words he brought Jesus out and seated him on the judge's bench in the place called Stone Pavement, in Hebrew, Gabbatha. It was preparation day for Passover, and it was about noon. And he said to the Jews, "Behold, your king!" They cried out, "Take him away, take him away! Crucify him!" Pilate said to them, "Shall I crucify your king?" The chief priests answered, "We have no king but Caesar." Then he handed him over to them to be crucified.

So they took Jesus, and, carrying the cross himself, he went out to what is called the Place of the Skull, in Hebrew, Golgotha. There they crucified him, and with him two others, one on either side, with Jesus in the middle. Pilate also had an inscription written and put on the cross. It read, "Jesus the Nazorean, the King of the Jews." Now many of the Jews read this inscription, because the place where Jesus was crucified was near the city; and it was written in Hebrew, Latin, and Greek. So the chief priests of the Jews said to Pilate, "Do not write 'The King of the Jews,' but that he said, 'I am the King of the Jews.'" Pilate answered, "What I have written, I have written."

APRIL 3 — FRIDAY OF THE PASSION OF THE LORD (GOOD FRIDAY) (CONTINUED)

When the soldiers had crucified Jesus, they took his clothes and divided them into four shares, a share for each soldier. They also took his tunic, but the tunic was seamless, woven in one piece from the top down. So they said to one another, "Let's not tear it, but cast lots for it to see whose it will be," in order that the passage of Scripture might be fulfilled that says:

They divided my garments among them,
and for my vesture they cast lots.

This is what the soldiers did. Standing by the cross of Jesus were his mother and his mother's sister, Mary the wife of Clopas, and Mary of Magdala. When Jesus saw his mother and the disciple there whom he loved he said to his mother, "Woman, behold, your son." Then he said to the disciple, "Behold, your mother." And from that hour the disciple took her into his home.

After this, aware that everything was now finished, in order that the Scripture might be fulfilled, Jesus said, "I thirst." There was a vessel filled with common wine. So they put a sponge soaked in wine on a sprig of hyssop and put it up to his mouth. When Jesus had taken the wine, he said, "It is finished." And bowing his head, he handed over the spirit.

[Here all kneel and pause for a short time.]

Now since it was preparation day, in order that the bodies might not remain on the cross on the sabbath, for the sabbath day of that week was a solemn one, the Jews asked Pilate that their legs be broken and that they be taken down. So the soldiers came and broke the legs of the first and then of the other one who was crucified with Jesus. But when they came to Jesus and saw that he was already dead, they did not break his legs, but one soldier thrust his lance into his side, and immediately blood and water flowed out. An eyewitness has testified, and his testimony is true; he knows that he is speaking the truth, so that you may come to believe. For this happened so that the Scripture passage might be fulfilled: Not a bone of it will be broken. *And again another passage says:* They will look upon him whom they have pierced.

After this, Joseph of Arimathea, secretly a disciple of Jesus for fear of the Jews, asked Pilate if he could remove the body of Jesus. And Pilate permitted it. So he came and took his body. Nicodemus, the one who had first come to him at night, also came bringing a mixture of myrrh and aloes weighing about one hundred pounds. They took the body of Jesus and bound it with burial cloths along with the spices, according to the Jewish burial custom. Now in the place where he had been crucified there was a garden, and in the garden a new tomb, in which no one had yet been buried. So they laid Jesus there because of the Jewish preparation day; for the tomb was close by.

Second Station: Jesus takes up the cross

John 19:13–17

Third Station: Jesus falls for the first time

Isaiah 53:4–7; John 1:29

Lamentations 1:12; Luke 2:25–40; John 19:26–27

 # Fifth Station: Simon of Cyrene helps Jesus carry His cross

Mark 8:34; Mark 15:21; 2 Timothy 2:3

Sixth Station: Veronica wipes the face of Jesus

Isaiah 53:2–3; Matthew 25:40

Seventh Station: Jesus falls the second time

Psalm 38:6–22; Isaiah 63:9

Eighth Station: Jesus consoles the women of Jerusalem

Matthew 7:21; Luke 23:27–31

Ninth Station: Jesus falls the third time

Psalm 37:23–24; Hebrews 4:15–16

Tenth Station: Jesus is stripped of His garments

Psalm 22:16–18; John 19:23–24

Eleventh Station: Jesus is nailed to the cross

Luke 23:33–43; John 19:1

Twelfth Station: Jesus dies on the cross

Matthew 27:50; John 19:28–37

Thirteenth Station: Jesus is taken down from the cross

Psalm 22:14–15; John 19:38–40

Fourteenth Station: Jesus is laid in the tomb

Matthew 27:57–61; Mark 15:46–47

After meditating upon the images of the Passion of the Lord, select one image which struck your heart. Spend time quietly looking at the image. Write down what Jesus says to You in this image.

_____
_____
_____
_____
_____
_____

✝ Longinus — the centurion

According to legend, Longinus was the Roman centurion (soldier) who pierced the side of Jesus with a lance while he was on the Cross and professed his belief in the Son of God. "When the centurion who stood facing him saw how he breathed his last he said, 'Truly this man was the Son of God!'" (Mark 15:17). The piercing of the side of Christ is the last act of the five Holy Wounds of Christ.

The five holy wounds of Christ are 1) nailing to cross through right hand, 2) nailing to cross through left hand, 3) nailing to cross through right food, 4) nailing to cross through left foot, 5) piercing of the side by the Holy Lance of Longinus. Jesus suffered other wounds during the passion, crown of thorns as well as scourging at the pillar.

It is believed that he converted to Christianity after witnessing the crucifixion. Longinus is venerated in the Roman Catholic Church, Eastern Orthodox Church, the Armenian Apostolic Church, and several other Christian churches.

Further reference: Louis de Wohl has authored two historical fiction novels which portray Longinus, *The Spear* and *The Glorious Folly*.

Gaze at the picture of the Roman soldier piercing the side of Christ on the back cover.

APRIL 4 — HOLY SATURDAY AT THE EASTER VIGIL IN THE HOLY NIGHT OF EASTER

A reading from an ancient homily for Holy Saturday

"What is happening? Today there is a great silence over the earth, a great silence, and stillness, a great silence because the King sleeps; the earth was in terror and was still, because God slept in the flesh and raised up those who were sleeping from the ages. God has died in the flesh, and the underworld has trembled.

Truly he goes to seek out our first parent like a lost sheep; he wishes to visit those who sit in darkness and in the shadow of death. He goes to free the prisoner Adam and his fellow-prisoner Eve from their pains, he who is God, and Adam's son.

The Lord goes in to them holding his victorious weapon, his cross. When Adam, the first created man, sees him, he strikes his breast in terror and calls out to all: 'My Lord be with you all.' And Christ in reply says to Adam: 'And with your spirit.' And grasping his hand he raises him up, saying: 'Awake, O sleeper, and arise from the dead, and Christ shall give you light.

'I am your God, who for your sake became your son, who for you and your descendants now speak and command with authority those in prison: Come forth, and those in darkness: Have light, and those who sleep: Rise.

'I command you: Awake, sleeper, I have not made you to be held a prisoner in the underworld. Arise from the dead; I am the life of the dead. Arise, O man, work of my hands, arise, you who were fashioned in my image. Rise, let us go hence; for you in me and I in you, together we are one undivided person.

'For you, I your God became your son; for you, I the Master took on your form; that of slave; for you, I who am above the heavens came on earth and under the earth; for you, man, I became as a man without help, free among the dead; for you, who left a garden, I was handed over to Jews from a garden and crucified in a garden.

'Look at the spittle on my face, which I received because of you, in order to restore you to that first divine inbreathing at creation. See the blows on my cheeks, which I accepted in order to refashion your distorted form to my own image.

'See the scourging of my back, which I accepted in order to disperse the load of your sins which was laid upon your back. See my hands nailed to the tree for a good purpose, for you, who stretched out your hand to the tree for an evil one.

APRIL 4 — HOLY SATURDAY AT THE EASTER VIGIL IN THE HOLY (CONTINUED)

"I slept on the cross and a sword pierced my side, for you, who slept in paradise and brought forth Eve from your side. My side healed the pain of your side; my sleep will release you from your sleep in Hades; my sword has checked the sword which was turned against you."

'But arise, let us go hence. The enemy brought you out of the land of paradise; I will reinstate you, no longer in paradise, but on the throne of heaven. I denied you the tree of life, which was a figure, but now I myself am united to you, I who am life. I posted the cherubim to guard you as they would slaves; now I make the cherubim worship you as they would God.'

"The cherubim throne has been prepared, the bearers are ready and waiting, the bridal chamber is in order, the food is provided, the everlasting houses and rooms are in readiness; the treasures of good things have been opened; the kingdom of heaven has been prepared before the ages."

Spend time looking at the painting. Describe the contrast between the demons and those whom Christ is leading to paradise.

_____

_____

_____

The Descent into Limbo, 1442 (fresco), Angelico, Fra (Guido di Pietro) / Museo di San Marco dell'Angelico, Florence, Italy / Bridgeman Images

The Resurrection, illustration for *The Life of Christ*, Tissot, James Jacques Joseph / Brooklyn Museum of Art, New York, USA / Bridgeman Images

APRIL 5

THE RESURRECTION OF THE LORD THE MASS OF EASTER SUNDAY

JOHN 20:1-9

On the first day of the week, Mary of Magdala came to the tomb early in the morning, while it was still dark, and saw the stone removed from the tomb. So she ran and went to Simon Peter and to the other disciple whom Jesus loved, and told them, "They have taken the Lord from the tomb, and we don't know where they put him." So Peter and the other disciple went out and came to the tomb. They both ran, but the other disciple ran faster than Peter and arrived at the tomb first; he bent down and saw the burial cloths there, but did not go in. When Simon Peter arrived after him, he went into the tomb and saw the burial cloths there, and the cloth that had covered his head, not with the burial cloths but rolled up in a separate place. Then the other disciple also went in, the one who had arrived at the tomb first, and he saw and believed. For they did not yet understand the Scripture that he had to rise from the dead.

Jesus Appears to the Holy Women, illustration from *The Life of Our Lord Jesus Christ*, Tissot, James Jacques Joseph / Brooklyn Museum of Art, New York, USA / Purchased by Public Subscription / Bridgeman Images

NOTES